THE

LIFE

OF

HARMAN BLENNERHASSETT

COMPRISING

AN AUTHENTIC NARRATIVE OF THE

Burr Expedition:

AND CONTAINING

MANY ADDITIONAL FACTS NOT HERETOFORE PUBLISHED.

BY

WILLIAM H. SAFFORD.

CINCINNATI:
MOORE, ANDERSON, WILSTACH & KEYS,
28 WEST FOURTH STREET.
1853.

STEREOTYPED BY L. JOHNSON AND CO.
PHILADELPHIA.

THE LIFE OF HARMAN BLENNERHASSETT

COMPRISING

AN AUTHENTIC NARRATIVE OF THE

Burr Expedition:

AND CONTAINING

MANY ADDITIONAL FACTS NOT HERETOFORE PUBLISHED.

BY

WILLIAM H. SAFFORD.

CINCINNATI:
MOORE, ANDERSON, WILSTACH & KEYS,
28 WEST FOURTH STREET.
1853.

STEREOTYPED BY L. JOHNSON AND CO.
PHILADELPHIA.

PREFACE.

WHILE collecting materials for the present biography, I have met with unexpected difficulties in procuring authentic information from the contemporaries of Blennerhassett. This is to be accounted for in the plain simplicity of most of his neighbours, who took but little interest in his scientific pursuits—of which they could neither understand the philosophy, nor comprehend the meaning. The consequence was, they associated but little with the man, and their acquaintance was derived more from what they saw, than from what they heard.

It gives me pleasure to acknowledge the courtesy of Dr. S. P. HILDRETH, of Marietta, in permitting me the use of the various historical incidents which his assiduity and love of the curious have rescued from oblivion. From the Blennerhassett Papers, published by WILLIAM WALLACE, Esq., I have made liberal quotations. To Maj. HORACE NYE, of Putnam, and Col.

Joseph Barker, of Newport, I am alike indebted for much valuable matter—rendered more interesting from the fact that they were eye-witnesses of some of the scenes I have attempted to describe. Others have furnished me with materials; but the multiplicity of their names must excuse their non-appearance.

I have been careful to introduce nothing, as fact, but what has been fully corroborated by living witnesses. Nor have I attempted to screen from the public eye the infirmities or faults of the subjects of these pages; while, at the same time, I can truly say, their virtues have not been exaggerated.

The work is now submitted to a charitable public, with a knowledge of its many imperfections. More skilful hands might have avoided many faults with which I am justly chargeable, and rendered it far more palatable to the reading critic.

The Author.

CONTENTS.

CHAPTER I.

CHAPTER II.

CHAPTER III.

CHAPTER IV.

CHAPTER V.

CHAPTER VI.

CHAPTER VII.

CHAPTER VIII.

CHAPTER IX.

CHAPTER X.

CHAPTER XI.

CHAPTER XII.

CHAPTER XIII.

CHAPTER XIV.

CHAPTER XV.

APPENDIX.

INTRODUCTION.

NEARLY fifty years since, the inhabitants of the valley of the Ohio were gratified by the intelligence that an individual of rank and fortune had renounced allegiance to his father-land, to take up his abode among them. In those primitive days, every addition to the little band of early pioneers was deemed of some importance; but the accession of one whose manners and customs differed so widely from their own—who could build and adorn a palace in the western wilds—was considered an event of wonderful magnitude.

With satisfaction they beheld the first germs of civilization springing from beneath the plastic hand of taste, and bursting into full maturity through the genial influence of wealth. This western Eden, while it captivated their eyes with its beauty, amazed their minds with the resources of its possessor. They witnessed the accomplishment of his ends in the subjugation of nature to his will; saw "the desert bloom and blossom as the rose;" stood as anxious spectators when the whirlwind of popular prejudice and passion prostrated the hopes and blasted the happiness of his household; and wept for the desolation which succeeded.

Since the celebrated expedition of Aaron Burr, the earlier fortunes of Blennerhassett have been the subject of singular curiosity. Many have been the surmises as to the causes which led the descendant of European nobility, to renounce the hereditary honours consequent upon family, for the secluded life of an unpretending republican. Some attribute it to an early alliance with a lady whose fortune and rank were unequal to those of his own; others to a want of success as a member of the Irish bar; while the uncharitable are anxious to throw around the subject conjectures of the darkest character.

The mystery which surrounds him and his "island home" has served, for more than forty years, to entertain the passing traveller, as, upon the bosom of the Ohio, the latter glides by the spot where once stood the American Alhambra. The marvellous stories of Spain—of Moslem enchantment and Moorish gold—are scarce less credible than the tales at such times repeated to the attentive ear of the listener.

Memory reverts with fond delight to the earlier days of our youthful pastimes, when, strolling through the embowered coppices of the isle, seated beneath the vine-clad cotton-tree, or gathering pebbles on the beach, the stern realities of life were forgotten; and, in the wild exuberance of our youthful fancy, we breathed to the image of our heart's first love the language of impassioned adoration. Around the name of Blennerhassett, and every thing connected with it, was waved the enchanting wand of romance; and tales of beauty, of splendour, and of crime, while they fascinated us with their witchery, startled us with his deep and dark designs.

Who Blennerhasset truly was, and what his origin and destiny, it is our object to disclose. We hope to strip the subject of that mysteriousness which ignorance, wilful prejudice, or a love of the marvellous has thrown around it, and reveal to the inquiring reader the acts and character of the man.

LIFE OF BLENNERHASSETT.

CHAPTER I.

Early life of Blennerhassett—Lineage—Education—The Irish bar—Blennerhassett commences the study of law—Called to the bar—Certificate—Makes a visit upon the Continent—France—Witnesses the adoption of her new Constitution—Returns to Ireland—Spirit of discontent in Ireland—Oppressed by England—Effect of the American Revolution on Ireland—On the whole of Europe—Repeal of the statute of sixth George First—Blennerhassett prefers the quiet pursuits of literature to the political arena—Is dissatisfied with Ireland, and determines to leave—Disposes of his lands—Proceeds to England—Addresses Miss Agnew—Marries—Reflections.

Of the early life of Blennerhassett we know, and therefore shall say, but little. That he was the son of an Irish gentleman, and was born in Hampshire, England, while the family were on a temporary visit to some friend or relative, in the year 1767, we are authentically informed. He might have boasted a lineage, which, although not *noble*, was, nevertheless, among the most illustrious of the Irish gentry.* Whether the boy ever exhibited any thing above the capacity of boys of his age,—or whether, on the contrary, he was considered a silent, dull, and uninteresting youth,—we know not; but that he enjoyed most excellent literary advantages, is clearly established by the fact that, at early age, he was placed by his father in the celebrated school of Westminster; that, after he had struggled, in honourable emulation, with the many worthies who have since so brilliantly adorned both the English and Irish nations, he was entered at Trinity College, Dublin, where he graduated, with honour to himself and credit to his professors.

At that time the Irish bar—a body formidable to the then existing government, by their

* Dr. S. P. Hildreth, in a Sketch of the Life of Blennerhassett, published in the "American Review," in 1848, states that Blennerhassett was of "*noble* descent." William Wallace, Esq., on the contrary, who had access to a portion of his papers, and who also published a sketch of the same individual, in the same periodical, in the year 1845, describes his parentage as among the most distinguished of the *gentry* of Ireland, who could trace their lineage as far back as the English King John. "The family consisted of branches located in the counties of Cork and Kerry. Many of the ancient heads were the chiefs of Balaceady Castle, and held numerous important offices. The subject of this sketch belonged to the Balaceady branch." I have chosen to adopt Mr. Wallace as, perhaps, the best informed author on this point, he having had access to some of Blennerhassett's papers, through the courtesy of a son of the latter.

character and capacity—comprised many sons of the resident noblemen and commoners of Ireland. The legal science was not then a mere *trade*, but a *profession*, requiring both learning and time to master its abstruse truths. Eloquence was looked upon as a qualification for the higher duties of the senate, and almost every peer and commoner had a relative enrolled among the number.

That Blennerhassett should remain an exception to the general custom, was hardly to be expected; and, accordingly, we find him snugly ensconced in the King's Inns as an entered apprentice in the study of the law. How successfully he waded through the musty tomes of black letter, which crowd that ancient library, is evidenced by the significant appendage of LL.D., which occasionally accompanied his name.

At Michaelmas term, in 1790, he was called to the bar, as is shown by the following certificate:*—

"King's Inns. These are to certify, that Harman Blennerhassett, Esq., was, in Michaelmas term, in the year of our Lord, one thousand seven hundred and ninety, generally admitted

* Wallace.

into the Honourable Society of the King's Inns, and called to the degree of Barrister therein. IN TESTIMONY whereof, I have hereunto affixed the seal of said Society this eighteenth day of November, in the year of our Lord one thousand seven hundred and ninety-five.

"WM. CALDBECK, *Treas.* [L.S.]

"Witness, *John Cook, Sub-Treas.*"

Blennerhassett declined entering upon the duties of his profession until he had made a tour upon the continent.

France then presented, both to the philosopher and politician, superior attractions over any of her sister kingdoms. At the period of Blennerhassett's visit she had been rocked by the whirlwind of revolution; and the established despotism of her military monarchs had been crumbled into atoms. The massive structure of the Bastile, which had stood four hundred years, every stone of which was wet with the tears and echoed the groans of four centuries of oppression, had been torn from its summit to its foundation, by the infuriated advocates of popular freedom. On the anniversary of its destruction, Louis Sixteenth, with thirty thousand delegates from the confederated National Guards of the kingdom, in the presence of five hundred thousand of their countrymen, had taken the oath of fidelity to the nation, to the Constitution, and, all save the monarch himself, to the king. But France was still trembling from the convulsions of her people. Her recuperating energies were starting afresh, on a new system of government, which had not yet gained either the confidence or affection of her subjects. Having witnessed the adoption of these new measures, with doubts of their ultimate success, Blennerhassett returned to his own country, in time to escape the storm which prostrated the hopes of the friends of the new constitution, and destroyed the life of the unfortunate Louis.

The same spirit of discontent which prevailed in France had extended to Ireland. For centuries had she groaned under the oppression of successive English monarchs. Her submission to the sceptres of Henry and of Richard had been construed into the *right* of *conquest;* and they sought to crush the native spirit of her people, by fomenting discord and exercising tyranny. Ireland had been blessed with a genial soil. Nature had lavished her brightest gifts upon her. The native character of her population was not inferior to that of other nations. But, of what avail were fertile fields, or gigantic intellects and towering talent, when national disorganization and political faction perverted the gifts of Providence to selfish purposes, or destroyed their usefulness, in the general wreck of distracted governments and divided subjects? Her manufacturing interest and commercial enterprise struggled long against the monopoly of England; but the superior power of her ruler enabled her to check their prosperity, by the heavy hand of arbitrary restraint. A deplorable want of union of sentiment and firmness of purpose, at all times prevented a successful separation from her powerful oppressor; and every attempt to claim her independence proved vain and abortive.

Thus, for ages, has Ireland, as the captive in his gloomy cell, awaked at times as from a troubled dream, to behold, with longing eyes, the dawn of the day of her emancipation; but, finding the darkness still prevailing, gave herself again to slumber, that she might the more readily forget her situation.

England, fearful of her growing strength, sought to subdue her spirit, by onerous exactions, and denying her the privilege of a free legislature. Not only against Ireland had she exercised her arbitrary will, but also against the colonies of her planting in North America. Vain in the conceit of her imperial power, she dared to exact obedience from peoples separated by the wide Atlantic, and command the same submission with which the oppressed subjects of Ireland had yielded. While her experimental philosophy had taught her that to retain her authority she must exercise tyranny, she had not reflected that there was a point in the system of her oppression, where submission to the will of an unyielding despot ceased to be a virtue.

The spirit of independence was hovering over the bloody altar of the American Revolution, when Ireland again awoke to a sense of her own condition. She gazed with animated delight at the increasing success of American arms. Every new victory found a sympathetic influence, responding with joy, in the secret recesses of her own bosom. The feeble colonies of America, spread over a vast extent of territory, with but few facilities for conducting a war; with a hostile Indian enemy in their rear, and the boasted chivalry of England at their front; undismayed by difficulty or the fear of defeat, after seven years of war, were finally victorious. The arrogance of England bowed its proud head to the shrine of liberty; and Lord Cornwallis, her favourite general, led back the relics of her conquered army, to commemorate, in the mother country, the importance of her power, and the emancipation of her colonies.

Before they had well considered the reason of their solicitude, the same spirit of independence had animated the Irish bosom; and, in every corner of her territory, the fire of liberty burst forth, in a blaze that threatened equal destruction to British usurpation and kingly government. The nation became aroused. English influence and English interests secured partisans in church and state; and opposing factions, from their intolerance and party animosity, had already commenced the Irish revolution.

The success of the cause of liberty in the American colonies, affected, most sensibly, the whole of Europe. It appeared, indeed, as though the fiat had gone forth, that monarchies and despotisms were for ever to cease from among men. "Strange and unforeseen events were crowding the annals of the world;—the established axioms of general polity began to lose their weight among nations;—and governments, widely wandering from the fundamental principles of their own constitutions, appeared carelessly travelling the road to ruin."

Such was the state of Europe; presenting an aspect not unlike that upon which we, of later days, have gazed, (and to which we still look, with feelings of solicitude and hope,) when Blennerhassett left the unhappy shores of France, for those, not less miserable, of his native country.

Ireland, it is true, from the helpless situation of England, at a time when her foreign wars and hapless defeats had exhausted the resources of that powerful nation, had successfully demanded the repeal of the statute of sixth George First, entitled "An Act for the better securing the dependency of the kingdom of Ireland upon the crown of Great Britain;" but her situation was not less distracted than before.

Although it was difficult to keep aloof from the entangling snares of party strife, Blennerhassett chose rather to pursue the more flowery paths of literature than the sterner and more rugged way of political preferment. To a mind which sought within itself for sources of enjoyment, the bustle and hurricane which reigned around served to distract his meditations, and interrupt the pleasure which, in seclusion, he had hoped to find.

Being the possessor of an estate, with considerable additional fortune inherited at the death of his father, he determined no longer to remain in Ireland, subjected to the inconvenience and danger which usually attend the feuds of faction; but, in some more remote and peaceful region, where the noise of the infuriated mob and war's dread clamour were never heard, he hoped to spend a life of repose.

He accordingly disposed of his lands to his relative, Baron Ventry,* and made immediate preparation for departing. Having closed his business, he started for England, where his two married sisters—one the consort of Lord Kingsale, the other of Admiral De Courcy—at that time resided.†

While here he frequently met with, and finally became affianced to, a Miss Agnew, daughter of the Lieutenant-governor of the Isle of Man, and grand-daughter of the celebrated general of that name, who fell at the battle of Germantown. She was young, intelligent, and beautiful. Possessed of an uncommon degree of energy, linked to a temperament of romantic ardour, she listened, with captivated delight, to the fairy stories he repeated, of the far-off land in the Western World. It is not, therefore, a

---

* Those who have spoken of this gentleman before, in connection with Blennerhassett, erroneously style him *Lord* Ventry.

† In this statement I follow the lead of Dr. Hildreth and Mr. Wallace; but as Lord Kingsale was also Admiral De Courcy, I am of opinion there was but one "sister" implicated.

matter of surprise that she consented to join her destinies with his, in the relation of husband and wife; and, as the partner of his joys, and the solace of his cares, to say, as Ruth to Naomi: "Whither thou goest I will go; and where thou lodgest I will lodge; thy people shall be my people, and thy God my God. Where thou diest will I die, and there will I be buried."

Upon the precarious sea of life, almost without compass or chart, Blennerhassett had now launched his adventurous barque. The sudden truth flashed across his mind, that he, too, was an adventurer; not, however, for the gold of Peru, for discoveries in the material world, or the subjugation of a foreign power. Gold, and honour, and station, were already his: but these, compared to the revelation of truth in the great volume of nature, to the inquiring mind, which sought to unfold her hidden mysteries, were but as "sounding brass and tinkling cymbal."

To him, that sea appeared serene and safe, with no adverse winds to interrupt his onward course; while, in the dim distance of imagination, he descried that shore of sweet repose, where the deceit and treachery of man should never disturb the quietude of a mind at peace.

CHAPTER II.

Blennerhassett supplies himself with a library and philosophical apparatus—Ships for New York—Western country described—Blennerhassett sets out for the West—Pittsburgh—Mode of travelling—Marietta—Is desirous of building—Backus's Island—Blennerhassett concludes a purchase—Commences improvements—Island with its improvements—Reflections.

Having supplied himself, in London, with an extensive library and a philosophical apparatus, together with other materials deemed necessary for future use, Blennerhassett shipped for New York, in 1797, where he remained, for several months, to study the topography of the country, and the character of its inhabitants.

At that time, the territory west of the Alleghanies—particularly the valley of the Ohio and Mississippi—was comparatively a wilderness. The enterprise of the pioneer had driven, to more distant regions, the aborigines of the West. The occasional hamlet, with its few acres of cultivated ground, interrupted, at intervals, the "boundless contiguity of shade," and marked the abode of civilized and associated man. Villages, with rude habitations, here and there, broke the eternal silence of the forest, and presented, to the adventurous traveller, as cheering a prospect as an oasis in the desert. Through this vast solitude, the silvery current of the Ohio wended its way to the "father of waters." The innovating steamer had never yet ruffled its bosom, nor startled its inhabitants with the sound of its machinery. The deer browsed among the thick undergrowth of its bottoms; the fox sought shelter in its caves; and the blood-scented wolf howled his wail of hunger, from the adjacent hills. Lands of almost inexhaustible fertility skirted its margin, and isles of peculiar beauty decked its surface.

Captivated with various descriptions of the country, in company with his wife, Blennerhassett set out to seek this delightful land. Crossing the rugged barriers of the Alleghanies, then a tedious and difficult undertaking, they arrived at Pittsburgh, in the fall of 1797, where their eyes first rested on that river, which afterwards proved the theatre of their happiness, their deception, and their ruin. Here they obtained passage on a keel-boat, in those days the most comfortable mode of travelling on the western waters; and shortly arrived at Marietta, a town of greater importance than any other in the State of Ohio.

The population of this pleasantly-situated village was unusually intelligent and moral. The puritanical character of its earlier inhabitants gave a tone to society, which identifies the present generation with their fathers who repose in their beautiful cemetery.

Blennerhassett's time was pleasantly occupied during the winter in visiting the various families, and making occasional excursions through the neighbourhood, to select a site for a residence. Above the village, and within a convenient distance, is an eminence of considerable height, commanding an extensive view of the river and surrounding country. With this situation he was much pleased, and had almost determined to erect on its summit, a castle, after the manner of many in his native country, but the ascent being difficult, and the declivities too precipitous, he abandoned the idea, and sought a situation more easy of access.

The following spring, he concluded to purchase an island in the Ohio river, about two miles below Parkersburg, or the mouth of the Little Kanawha, which, to his peculiar mind, possessed superior advantages to the adjacent farm. To one of romantic temperament, its locality was truly delightful. Upon its gently-sloping banks waved the drooping branches of the willow, and laved their graceful foliage in the passing stream. The majestic forest trees, untouched by the hand of civilization, reared their tall trunks, as monarchs of the land; while the wild-brier and woodbine, blending in promiscuous profusion, entwined their tendrils around the shrubbery of the wild-wood. Flowers of rare beauty burst spontaneously from the soil, and mingled their fragrance with the passing breeze. The happy songsters of the woods warbled forth their lively notes in the secluded groves, until each bush and branch appeared vocal with the songs of nature's music.

Could the mind, in pursuit of seclusion and repose, picture to its imagination a situation more desirable? Here might his cultivated taste adorn, to every extent, the ruder touches of nature, and mellow into softer shades the harsher outlines of her pencil; here might the mind, unfettered from worldly cares, drink deeper draughts from Truth's ever-flowing fountain; here,

"At the shadowy close of day,
When the hushed grove has sung its parting lay;
When pensive Twilight, in her dusky car,
Comes slowly on, to meet the evening star,

Above, below, aerial murmurs swell,
From hanging wood, brown heath, and bushy dell;
A thousand nameless rills that shun the light;
Stealing soft music on the ear of night;
So oft the finer movements of the soul,
That shun the sphere of pleasure's gay control,
In the still shades of calm seclusion rise,
And breathe their sweet, seraphic harmonies."*

When fatigued with the severer studies of science, he could amuse himself with the traditions and stories of several intelligent revolutionary soldiers who resided on the Belpré shore; or, as game abounded, might engage in the delightful sports of hunting and fishing.

That portion of the island purchased by Blennerhassett, was known by the familiar cognomen of "Backus's Island," and contained about one hundred and seventy acres. General Washington, it is said, embraced this little gem of nature, in the many valuable tracts of land entered by him on the bottoms of the Ohio. His far-seeing eye proved as successful, in judging of the future advantages of his various locations, as of the material of men and soldiers.

In 1798, Blennerhassett, having purchased the upper portion of the island, at a cost of four thousand five hundred dollars, moved into a block-house situated near the head. This, to

---

* Rogers.

those who had enjoyed the splendour of palaces, with the many conveniences which the arts of civilization afford, was a sorrowful exchange, which few could desire, and fewer still would have made. He energetically commenced clearing the grounds of the thick growth of timber and underwood, for a site upon which to erect a dwelling. Many hands were requisite, in addition to the slaves he had recently purchased, for the laborious task. The forest trees were uprooted, and their boughs and trunks conveyed away. The small inequalities, not suiting his fastidious taste, were smoothed and regulated as fancy dictated.

Vainly ambitious to excel any private residence west of the mountains, and to fashion it after those of his own country, economy and simplicity were not consulted in its construction. The sum of sixty thousand dollars, it is said, was expended by Blennerhassett, in fully establishing himself in his new abode. To the mind of the voyager descending the river, as the edifice rose majestically in the distance, spreading its wings to either shore, the effect was magical; and emotions were produced, not unlike those experienced in gazing on the Moorish palaces of Andalusia. There was a spell of enchantment around it, which would fain induce the credulous to believe that it had been created by magic, and consecrated to the gods. On a nearer approach was observed the beautifully graded lawn, decked with tasteful shrubbery, and interspersed with showy flowers; while, a little in the distance, the elm threw its dark branches over a carpet of most beautiful green sward. Beyond these, the forest trees were intermingled with copse-wood, so closely as to exclude the noon-day sun; and, in other places, they formed those long sweeping vistas, in the intricacies of which the eye delights to lose itself; while the imagination conceives them as the paths of wilder scenes of sylvan solitude.

The space immediately in the rear of the dwelling was assigned to fruits and flowers; of which the varieties were rare, excellent and beautiful; and the manner in which they were disposed over the surface, unique, elegant and tasteful. Espaliers of peach, apricot, quince and pear trees, extended along the exterior, confined to a picket fence; while, in the middle space, wound labyrinthine walks, skirted with flowering shrubs, and the eglantine and honey-suckle flung their melliferous blossoms over bowers of various forms.

On the south was the vegetable garden; and, adjoining this, a thrifty young orchard, embracing many varieties of fruit—promising abundant supplies for future use. Not entirely neglecting the useful for the ornamental, Blennerhassett had cleared a hundred acres below, and cultivated, in great perfection, the various crops adapted to the soil.

"The hall was a spacious room, its walls painted a sombre colour, with a beautiful cornice of plaster, bordered with gilded moulding, running round the lofty ceiling; while its furniture was rich, heavy and grand. The furniture in the drawing-room was, in strong contrast with that of the hall, light, airy and elegant; with splendid mirrors, gay-coloured carpets, classic pictures, rich curtains, and ornaments to correspond, arranged, by Mrs. Blennerhassett, with nicest taste and harmonious effect. A large quantity of silver-plate ornamented the sideboards and decorated the tables. The whole establishment was chastened by the purest taste, and without that glare of tinsel finery, too common among the wealthy."

Such was the residence of Blennerhassett, after he had expended much labour and money to render it the reality of what before was but ideal, an image of which had long haunted his dreams of youthful fancy, as the picture of sylvan beauty, of peaceful solitude, and of calm repose. How marked the mutations of a few short years! Ireland, but as yesterday, claimed him as a representative of one of her great families and of her constitution. The deference, due alike to rank and birth, in a monarchical government, was his by inheritance; and the favour of courts and of coronets was obtained without an effort, and resigned without control. Around him, a restless and distracted population were daily enacting scenes of outrage and oppression; and the hand of civilization, while it gave energy to intellect and advanced the arts and sciences, proved a powerful auxiliary in aggravating the causes and perpetuating the scenes of the revolution. To-day, we view him as the retired citizen of a republic, in the bosom of the forest of the Western World, with no tie of kindred, save the faithful companion of his bosom, and the two little sons who had been added to his household. Quietly retired from the busy haunts of man, his hours of study were only intruded upon by the friendly visits of his neighbours, to whose natures, dissimulation and flattery were alike unknown, and whose society and attachment he cherished by reciprocal attentions.

Amidst this peaceful solitude, how fully could he adopt the sentiment of the rural poet:—

"Welcome, pure thoughts! welcome, ye silent groves!
These guests, these courts, my soul most dearly loves;
How the wing'd people of the sky shall sing,
My cheerful anthem to the gladsome spring.
Here dwell no hateful looks—no palace cares,—
No broken vows dwell here, no pale-faced fears."

CHAPTER III.

Blennerhassett described—Studies—Amusements—Anecdotes of—Appointed justice of the peace—Mrs. Blennerhassett described.

Blennerhassett was about six feet in stature, of slender proportions, and slightly stooping. He was entirely devoid of that *suaviter in modo*, which is so attractive to the gentler sex, and not unfrequently captivates the minds of firmer mould, in society at large. His forehead, the index usually resorted to by which to judge of men's minds and measure the depth of intellect, was prominent, and claimed for its possessor, by the general rule, an intelligence above the ordinary capacity of mankind. His nose was the distinguishing feature of a face which wore an aspect of seriousness and thought, almost amounting to cold reserve. Like many of the nobility, he was extremely near-sighted; and, unlike many of the present age, who ape this defect of nature as characteristic of the aristocracy or the *literati*, he found it a matter of serious inconvenience. In gunning, particularly, (an amusement of which he was passionately fond,) he had usually to be accompanied by his wife, or some one of his servants, who levelled his fowling-piece and brought it to bear on the game. Peter, a domestic who sometimes attended him on such occasions, was in the habit of taking his station at a short distance, and giving directions after the following manner:—

"Now, level, Mr. Blennerhassett. A little to the left!—Now to the right!—there!—steady!—*fire!*"—Off would go the gun, and, not unfrequently, the game, likewise.

His usual dress was of the "old English style, with scarlet, or buff-coloured, small-clothes and silk stockings; shoes, with silver buckles; and a coat generally of blue broad-cloth. When at home, his dress was rather careless; often, in warm weather, in his shirt sleeves, without coat or waistcoat; and, in winter, he wore a thick woollen roundabout or jacket."*

Retiring in disposition, his life was sedentary and studious; books and philosophical experiments possessing greater attractions than the gay and fashionable assemblies of the ball-room. Always entertaining, he never indulged in

* Hildreth.—"American Review," 1848.

trivial conversation, but interested his audience in something calculated more to instruct than amuse their idle fancy.

His scientific studies, which were much facilitated by means of his various apparatus, included chemistry, electricity, galvanism, and astronomy. By the aid of a telescope and solar microscope, it was with much satisfaction that he could demonstrate the truth of his theories by practical observation, and acquaint himself more fully with the motions and positions of the various planets, as well as the minuter bodies of the earth. While experimenting in chemistry, he had conceived the idea that animal substance might be so adipocerated as to subserve the use of spermaceti for light. He accordingly placed pieces of meat in a small inlet from the river, to undergo a chemical change. When the proper time had elapsed, as he supposed, to test the truth of his theory, on visiting the cove he found the finny tribes of the water had anticipated his experiment by converting the meat into food. The act was not repeated, and his theory remained undemonstrated.

He was a connoisseur in music, and performed admirably upon the violin and violoncello. Many of his hours of recreation were whiled away with this delightful amusement; and, being an adept, pieces of his own composition were played with animating effect.

Of an unsuspecting disposition, he was easily imposed upon by the misrepresentations of others. Not unfrequently had he to pay enormously for his practical knowledge of life and human nature. It is reported of him that, on one occasion, having employed an individual to collect muscle shells from the beach, on which they were scattered in great profusion, when the labourer came to receive his pay, Blennerhassett inquired the reason of his high charge.

"The diving's so deep, and the shells are so scarce."

"But," replied Blennerhassett, "you do not dive, do you?"

"Ay, indeed! In fifteen feet water."

Believing there was no occasion for misrepresenting a fact, which could be readily ascertained by a short walk to the river, Blennerhassett paid the man his money—a sum equal to five times the real value of the shells.

Of a nervous temperament, he not unfrequently imagined objects which had no existence in nature, and apprehended evils that were never to be realized. Earthquakes and thunderstorms, to him, were intensely alarming; and such was his timidity on the approach of a threatening cloud, that it was his usual custom to close the doors and windows of his house, and place himself in the centre of a bed, to avoid the accidental effects of the electric fluid.

Of his forensic talents, or legal ability, he never, in this country, gave evidence. He was not deficient, however, in either. The county court of Wood county recommended him to the Governor of Virginia for the magistracy; and by His Excellency he was duly commissioned: but presuming it a condescension for which he should be poorlv paid, and still less respected, he modestly declined to "qualify," and remained a private citizen.

Let us turn, for a time, from the man, to contemplate and gaze upon the person and character of his companion. History affords but few instances where so much feminine beauty, physical endurance, and many social virtues, were combined with so brilliant a mind, in the person of a female.

Her stature was above the ordinary height of her sex; her form well-proportioned and beautifully symmetrical; her manners of the most captivating gracefulness, with sufficient dignity to repel familiarity and command respect. Her dark-blue eyes, beaming with love and affection, and "sparkling with life and intelligence," looked forth from beneath the long brown lashes, which hung as curtains to conceal their charms. Features of Grecian mould, embellished by a complexion whose carnation hue, health, and the hand of nature alone, had painted. Her hair, which was of a dark-brown colour, was usually concealed beneath a head-dress of rich coloured silk, worn after the manner of the Turkish turban.

Her mind was not less polished than her manners; and the fluency with which she wrote and spoke the French and Italian languages indicated a high degree of cultivation, which few, even in this golden age of science and letters, have ever attained to. Her taste for dramatic composition led her to adopt, as a favourite pastime, the rehearsal of Shakspeare's plays. These were usually executed with an effect which would have done honour to more professed connoisseurs, and exhibited a talent which needed only cultivation to have won laurels of lasting freshness in the theatrical world. Her familiarity with various French and English authors rendered her an agreeable companion for the man of letters, and proved a valuable assistant to her husband in recalling to mind some opinion or expression of an author which had escaped his memory.

She cultivated, to some extent, a taste for poetry, and produced several pieces which are still in existence. As we are enabled to offer a specimen of her powers in this flowery department of literature, we forbear an expression of opinion, but leave the lines to represent their authoress.*

But it is only in the every-day affairs of life that we can gain a perfect knowledge of the true character of individuals. It was in this peculiar sphere that Mrs. Blennerhassett exhibited an uncommon degree of excellence, and won the affection of all within her influence. She adapted her customs to the society around her, and joined in their amusements and festivities with all the spirit of one accustomed to frontier life from earliest infancy. Riding on horseback was a delightful and healthy exercise, in which she frequently participated. At such times, she was usually habited in a fine cloth riding-dress, of scarlet colour, richly bespangled with gold lace and glittering buttons. From her downy hat waved "the graceful plume of the ostrich," and the rich folds of her

---

* See Chap. XIII.

drapery fell gaily over the flanks of her noble steed. Over hill and through dale, with the fleetness of the deer, she took her course, and seldom did her attendant get a glimpse of his sprightly charge until she checked her speed to await his coming.

That she was capable of extraordinary physical endurance, was frequently demonstrated by the long and speedy walks she performed, whether on business or visiting some favourite friend. She has been known to accomplish a pedestrian tour, of from ten to twenty miles, with as much ease as other ladies would make their usual calls among city or village acquaintances. Fences or fallen timber were no impediments. Bounding over them with astonishing agility, she carelessly pursued her way, as though tracing the more familiar paths of the wild woods.

Although she participated in the various amusements through the country, and was the ruling spirit of every assembly, she never neglected the ordinary duties of her household; every apartment received her personal attention, from the kitchen to the chambers, and was duly cleansed and arranged according to her direction. By her were the daily tasks of the servants assigned, while she performed with cheerfulness the duties devolving on herself. In short, like Shakspeare's Portia,

"She was, indeed, a rich-souled creature, in whom the first germs of womanhood had blossomed forth, without a weed to check, or a chill to blight their growth."

CHAPTER IV.

Early settlers of Western Virginia—Occupations—Amusements—Patriotism—First settlers of Ohio—Industry—Economy—Morality—Conclusion.

THE character, manners, and habits of life of the early settlers of Western Virginia, are topics which have engaged the labours of but few pens; but they are not the less interesting on that account.

Many of the inhabitants of this new, and hitherto uncultivated portion of the State, were intelligent sons of families of distinction in the "Old Dominion." The great abundance of game of nearly every variety; the free and exciting sports of a life in the western wilds, devoid of care, and free from those conventional restraints which more polished society imposes on individuals, and by which, to a considerable extent, their actions are controlled; the exhilarating, health-invigorating, glorious fun of chasing

"The stag to the slippery crag,
And following the bounding roe;"—

combined to allure the ardent and pleasure-loving youths from the tamer scenes of their childhood to those boundless fields of new and ever-changing excitement. Others, enjoying smaller patrimonies, hearing of the rich alluvial bottoms of the Ohio and its tributaries, and the low price at which land could be procured, deserted their less-inviting homesteads to seek new sources of wealth beyond those blue peaks which many regarded as the western limit of civilization. Penury, and the exhausted lands of other portions of the State, drove no inconsiderable number in search of genial soil, where the hand of man might realize rich returns from the toil bestowed upon it; or the abounding game should furnish supplies of food without that effort which nature requires of those who seek her bounties.

Populated by these various classes, enticed thither through considerations as different as the dispositions and circumstances of the individuals themselves, that love of society which is seldom lost in man served to banish distinctions of rank, and render an absolute equality essentially necessary to their social existence. Around the blazing fire, the son of the wide-famed statesman tripped merrily in the misty mazes of the dance with the daughter of the unknown peasant. The scholar, orator, and divine strove in eager emulation to plant their rifle-balls as near the centre of the target as that of the uncultivated woodsman.

Remote from friends, from society, and the pleasing associations of earlier years, they devised amusements in every thing, and made frolic of labour itself. A house-raising, or log-rolling, was as cheerfully attended as the wedding of a favourite friend; and a corn-husking collected the inhabitants from several miles around. The almost daily interchange of civilities, and constant association of the various classes, as well for the purpose of joint protection against the deadly rifle of the savage, as the innate love of company, served to mould the general character of the population into a distinct type, peculiar to themselves, and stamped their virtues with an originality which the mutations of time have failed to change.

The Virginian, thus re-moulded, (if we may be allowed the expression,) from his active habits of life, was capable of extraordinary feats of strength and astonishing agility of limb. For a wrestle, or a foot-race, he was always ready, and never refused a challenge to take a trial at either. While, to gratify his revenge, he would have grappled with Apollo for the tripod of the temple; yet the overflowing fountains of his heart gushed forth, in swelling streams of sympathy, for the misfortunes of his fellow-men. Chivalrous, brave, and independent, "he would not have courted Neptune for his trident, nor Jove for his power to thunder." With a generosity bordering on extravagance, his house, his horse, his gun—yea, every thing but the sacredness of virtue were at the disposal of his friends. Clad in the buck-skin moccasin, with a hunting-shirt of linsey-woolsey, his rifle on his shoulder, and a butcher-knife at his side, he never changed his apparel to suit the circumstances under which he was placed; and, whether pursuing the fleeting game, visiting a neighbour, or attending the services of the church, the same attire was suitable both to the day and the occasion.

The deer hunt, the horse race, and ever-glorious fox-chase, were the usual sources of amusement among the men; while the women found enjoyment at the various wool-pickings and quiltings throughout the neighbourhood. The circumstance of their spending so much time, in the enjoyment of lawful amusements, is to be accounted for in the fact, that, at that early period, they had but few desires to be satisfied, and fewer wants to be supplied. There being then but little, if any, demand for agricultural produce, it was unnecessary to raise more than the consumption of the immediate vicinity required. Remotely situated from the extravagance and luxury of more cultivated society, there was no need of mahogany sideboards, groaning with champaign, nor of Brussels or Turkey carpets to decorate their floors.

Their unflinching patriotism was repeatedly tested in the Revolution, and various engagements with the Indians. At the first call of their country's voice, the animated response was heard in every hamlet. When they had neither the soldier's uniform, nor equipages, nor arms, they seized their trusty rifles; and, from their smiling fields of toil, from the pleasant scenes of their sportive pastimes, they flew to win a soldier's name or a soldier's grave. The results of their efforts shall glow beneath the pencil and the pen—shall live in national song, and survive in the spirit-stirring anthem, till none are worthy to repeat the strain, or to paint the scenes of their country's glory! When the question of the purchase of Louisiana was first mooted in our national councils, and it was then urged that the inhabitants of that territory would prevent a free and easy navigation of the Mississippi river;—"Give me," said Washington, "three hundred picked men, well-tried and true, of old West Augusta,* and I will *carve* my way to the Gulf." What higher compliment could have been paid to the patriotism and bravery of the original settlers of the trans-Alleghany country—a remnant of whom a few still remain, as land-marks by which to trace the characters of the departed!

While this type of character occupied the Eastern shore of the Ohio, that of the West contained another, as marked and distinct as that of the Cavalier from the Roundhead. Many revolutionary officers and soldiers of the Northern States, who had exhausted their resources in fighting the battles of their country, and who, from the depleted state of the national finances had to remain for a time without indemnity, either for their services or losses, sought this new land, where they could recuperate their shattered fortunes by economy and industry. Others, too, of the sons of New England, attracted also by the fruitful valleys of this beautiful and majestic river, bade farewell to the rocky and ungrateful soil of their birth, and, with a plough and a bed, a Bible and a wife,

* This was the term applied to all the territory west of the Alleghanies, known as the North-West Territory. Augusta County then comprising the whole.

set out for the West. Here, hundreds of miles from father Aminidab and mother Patience, they set themselves industriously to work, clearing up farms from which to realize fortunes, as soon as the circumstances of the country would permit. That their most sanguine expectations have been fully realized, is happily demonstrated by the fields waving with grain, valleys filled with herds, and hills covered with flocks, which meet the eye of the traveller as he passes along the stream. While the meed of praise has been awarded them for their indefatigable industry, they have not been regarded as possessing that generous hospitality which is characteristic of their neighbours of Virginia. Educated to believe there was no product without labour—no wealth without economy—they indulged but little in amusements, and were careful against expense. In their moral and religious observances, they were rigidly austere. Like the Puritans of Plymouth Rock, from whom they were descended, the Bible formed the chief rule of their conduct. Their family government was based upon its precepts, and its holy teachings were listened to each Sabbath, in the "forest sanctuary." True, some there were who occasionally broke over the more austere lessons which had been taught them by their parents, but the exceptions, "like angels' visits, were few and far between." If their liberality at any time exhibited itself, it was usually towards objects of charity, or to spread the teachings of that gospel which they had been taught ever to revere. For bravery and devotion to the welfare of their country, they were justly regarded the equals of their neighbours; and acts of Indian cruelty were jointly revenged by the two. Having enjoyed early advantages in the best schools and academies of their native States, they were fully informed upon the subjects usually taught at such institutions, and many possessed talents of superior brilliancy.

Such were the men with whom Blennerhassett had cast his fortunes. The variety of characters, perhaps, was as great, if the number of persons was far less, as that of the society he had recently abandoned. There was the hospitable Virginian, who, though he neither claimed nor desired the titulary dignity of a nobleman, exhibited a generosity equal to that of its proudest possessor,—a generosity which knew no bounds, and awaited no emergency for its exercise. With a reckless profligacy, he scattered his bounties broad-cast; threw open the doors of hospitality; lavishing, with an unsparing hand, the gifts which fortune had bestowed upon him. There was the high-toned chivalry of the Crusades, which stooped to no baseness; cringed to no superior; nor was intimidated by menace; performing kindnesses, without ostentation; acts of daring, without boasting, and relieving the wants of the distressed, without the hope of reward. There was the zealous Puritan, acknowledging no superior but God; no law binding on the moral man, but the Bible; no religion but that of Calvin; rejecting the unmeaning forms of Popery; combating the doctrine of apostolic succession; and discarding, in his worship, the use of the gown, the surplice, and the prayer-book. There, the meek and pious Christian, dispensing charities without parsimony; visiting the sick and the afflicted; and mingling the comforts of religion with the sad and agonizing scenes of death. And there, too, alas!—the crafty and wily miscreant, making promises never to be fulfilled; taking advantages in trade: regarding neither the teachings of Holy Writ, nor the precepts of morality; but ever faithless, ever insincere, prostrating virtue without compunction, and indulging in every lawless vice.

CHAPTER V.

Domestic situation of Blennerhassett in 1805—Burr's first visit to the island—Object of Burr's tour—Finds Blennerhassett absent from home—Proceeds down the Ohio—Visits Wilkinson—Conference—Blennerhassett visits New York—Thomas Addis Emmett—Burr's first communication to Blennerhassett—Effect of, upon Blennerhassett—Blennerhassett's answer—Burr's reply—Burr's second visit to the island—Wirt's description of the island as it was at that time—Burr commences recruiting men for the expedition—Arguments made use of to induce individuals to join—Effect of his arguments.

EIGHT years had already elapsed since Blennerhassett had made the island his residence. The flowers and shrubbery planted by his hands had now sprung up in luxuriant perfection, and regaled the senses with their grateful fragrance. The products of his husbandry secured at least a comfortable supply of all the necessaries of life, and more than this he wished not. The independence of his situation enabled him to procure any or all of the delicacies which a more Epicurean taste might have desired; but these had been resigned, with the pomp and glitter of his former station. Around him, he viewed a contented family, rejoicing in the buoyancy of health, and with the sprightliness of youthful vivacity. The returning seasons brought with them returning pleasures. New scenes of interest, new engagements, and wider fields of usefulness, daily presented themselves to his awakening impulses; but, in the midst of all this peace and cheerfulness—this "constant sunshine of the soul"—a dark and portentous cloud gathered in the horizon of his effulgent future, destined soon to burst with sad fatality upon the unsuspecting circle of that household.

In the spring of 1805, Aaron Burr, late Vice President of the United States, after the closing of the session of Congress, set out on a journey through the Western States. The object of this tour, although never definitively declared, was, doubtless, three-fold:—

First. To ascertain the sentiments of the people of the West upon the subject of a separation from the Atlantic States.

Secondly. To enlist recruits, and make arrangements for a private expedition against Mexico and the Spanish provinces, in the event of a war between the United States and Spain, which at that time seemed inevitable.

Thirdly. In the event of a failure of both of these measures, to purchase a tract of land of Baron Bastrop, lying in the territory of Louisiana, on the Washita river. Upon this, he contemplated the establishment of a colony of intelligent and wealthy individuals, where he might rear around him a society remarkable for its refinement in civil and social life. That each of these stupendous enterprises was determined on, is clearly inferable from the evidence afterward adduced against him.

With a mind, tortured by remorse for the unfortunate duel with Hamilton; sickened by disappointment in political preferment; disgusted with the more pacific measures of Jefferson, he could only direct his thoughts in scenes of outward conflict, and bury the disquietudes which were tearing his soul, by plunging into deeds of wonderful magnitude.

Knowing full well the advantages which wealth and influence would add to either undertaking, he sought first to secure the co-operation of the most conspicuous characters at that time occupying the West. Blennerhassett was a shining treasure, too valuable to remain unnoticed:—a gentleman of opulence and ease, possessing a mind of superior scientific acquirements; and who, from the discontents of his own country, it would readily be presumed, was well acquainted with military tactics; such a personage would indeed prove a powerful auxiliary in any measure he had proposed to himself. Burr, accordingly, landed at the island; and, in company with a Mrs. Shaw, strolled over this far-famed paradise. Mr. Blennerhassett was absent from home. His wife's attention having been attracted by the strangers who were then surveying the premises, she despatched a messenger to them, tendering the hospitalities of the mansion. To increase her surprise, Burr returned his card by the servant, stating that as curiosity alone had prompted the visit, they must decline the invitation. Honoured by the attention of so distinguished an individual as the Ex-Vice-President of the United States, Mrs. Blennerhassett was unusually importunate; and Burr, with an assumption of hesitation, finally yielded.

Having participated in the general topics of conversation, until about eleven o'clock at night, Burr re-embarked on board of his boat, and proceeded down the river, to view the country and hold conferences with the inhabitants at the various points.

General Wilkinson, who commanded the western forces, was, at that time, temporarily at

Fort Massac, near the mouth of the Ohio. As a previous correspondence had been held between them, which had brought them into intimate relations, Burr wished to ascertain, with what confidence he could rely on the aid of that officer and his men, in the event of an expedition to Mexico. The result of that interview has never been definitely ascertained; but it was strongly suspected, however, that Wilkinson assured him of his support. Here, the Ex-Vice-President was furnished by the general, with an elegant barge, sails, colours and ten oars, with a sergeant and ten able hands to prosecute his journey.

About this time, Blennerhassett, having received intelligence of the arrival, in New York, of his classmate and friend, the celebrated Thomas Addis Emmett, who had been compelled to flee his country, by reason of serious political difficulties, hastened to meet him. The feelings of the exiles, as they again clasped hands on the western borders of the Atlantic, can only be fully appreciated by those who have experienced the emotions. Here he found one with whom he could freely sympathize, and who, in return, could as freely sympathize with him. Often, in early life, had they sported together over the same green meadows, and participated in the same amusements. And when, at a more advanced age, they had been honourable competitors for academic honours, no selfish ambition had served to unloose the bonds which early childhood welded, although the contest was never so spirited, or the prize was never so dazzling. Still later in life, they had deplored together the fate of their country; had witnessed her deep degradation, and sighed over the hopeless prospects which were shadowed in the distant future. After several weeks spent with his friend, during which time he renewed his former acquaintance in the city, he returned to his family on the island.

In the beginning of December, 1805, Burr addressed a communication to Blennerhassett, regretting that the absence of the latter had deprived the former of the pleasure of improving his personal acquaintance, when visiting his island residence. In an insinuating but guarded manner, he alluded to the talents of Blennerhassett, as deserving of a higher sphere than that in which they were employed. He was surrounded, to be sure, with all the comforts of life, but those very comforts only served to effeminate the mind, for want of active engagements. His pleasures were merely passive, and were better suited to the negative enjoyment of the rude and unconscious herd, than to those delightful sensations experienced by the intelligent mind when in the active exercise of all its ennobling powers. There were other considerations, too, which should induce him to feel that *physical* effort was necessary. He was surrounded by a growing family, who demanded of him superior advantages over those to be obtained in his new and unpolished neighbourhood. His fortune was gradually diminishing, while no effort was made to add to his present estate. The inevitable consequence therefore must be the impoverishment of his children by his listless attention to all financial affairs. Suggesting several plans by which Blennerhassett might enhance his fortune, and render himself a more important individual in society, he left him to meditate on the truthfulness of the picture so dexterously set before him.

Such apparently disinterested counsel, from one whose judgment and experience he respected, caused Blennerhassett to turn his attention, more particularly than he had hitherto done, towards himself and his own affairs. The result was all that Burr could have desired. An answer was returned, in which the writer desired to be admitted into a participation of any speculation which might present itself to Burr's judgment as worthy to engage his talents. "In making this advance," says Blennerhassett, "I contemplated not only a commercial enterprise or land purchase, but a military adventure was distinctly mentioned in which I would engage." He said, he conceived the country on the eve of a Spanish war, when it would be necessary to call all the talents of the country into action, among which, the brightest was Burr's, and under such considerations he was willing to engage in any enterprise for the subjugation of the Spanish dominion.*

To this communication the following reply was returned :—

"WASHINGTON CITY, April 15th, 1806.

"DEAR SIR :—Your very interesting letter, of the 21st December, arrived here just after I had passed through this city on my way to South Carolina, and was not received until about two months after its date. The subject of it" [securing land in the South-West,] "has been daily in my mind. Independently of considerations personal to myself, I learn, with the utmost pleasure, that you are to be restored to the social and the active world. Your talents and

* See Blennerhassett's Brief: Appendix, No. 4.

acquirements seemed to have destined you for something more than vegetable life; and, since the first hour of our acquaintance, I have considered your seclusion as a fraud on society. The confidence you have seen fit to place in me is extremely flattering, and it would seem that there has been, without explanation, a sort of consent between our minds. In a matter of so much moment, and on which I am so imperfectly informed, it would be hazarding too much to offer advice, yet it is due to the frankness of your letter, to acknowledge that I had projected, and still meditate, [partly obliterated] a speculation precisely of the character you have described. It would have been submitted to your consideration, in October last, if I had then had the good fortune to find you at home. The business, however, in some degree depends on contingencies not within my control, and will not be commenced before December, if ever. From this circumstance, and as the matter in its present state cannot be satisfactorily explained by letter, the communication will be deferred till a personal interview can be had. With this view, I pray to be informed of your intended movements the ensuing season, and in case you should visit Orleans, at what time and what port you may be expected on the Atlantic coast. But I must insist that these intimations be not permitted to interrupt the prosecution of any plans which you have formed for yourself. No occupation which will not take you off the continent can interfere with that which I may propose." [The letter then gives an account of the society of Orleans, and concludes:] "We shall have no war" [with Spain], "unless we should be actually invaded. Some estimate of the views and temper of our government may be formed from the proceedings of the House of Representatives with closed doors. A copy of that part of their journal I sent for your amusement.

"Accept, dear sir, assurances of the great consideration and respect, with which

"I am, your obedient servant,

A. BURR."*

"*H. Blennerhassett, Esq.*"

In the month of August, 1806, Burr, accompanied by his accomplished daughter, Mrs. Theodosia Alston, wife of Gov. Joseph Alston of South Carolina,† visited the island. As this interview has been eloquently alluded to by the distinguished William Wirt, it is introduced as

* "Blennerhassett;" By Wm. Wallace: "American Review," 1845.

† See Appendix No. 1.

descriptive of the domestic situation of the Blennerhassett family, at this particular period. He remarks :—

"A shrubbery, which Shenstone might have envied, blooms around him; music that might have charmed Calypso and her nymphs, is his; an extensive library spreads its treasures before him; a philosophical apparatus offers to him all the mysteries and secrets of nature; peace, tranquillity and innocence shed their mingled delights around him; and, to crown the enchantment of the scene, a wife who is said to be lovely even beyond her sex, and graced with every accomplishment that can render it irresistible, has blessed him with her love, and made him the father of her children. The *evidence* would convince you, that this is only a faint picture of real life. In the midst of all this peace, this innocence, this tranquillity, this feast of mind, this pure banquet of the heart, the destroyer comes :—he comes to turn his paradise into a hell;—yet the flowers do not wither at his approach, and no monitory shuddering, through the bosom of their unfortunate possessor, warns him of the ruin that is coming upon him. A stranger presents himself. Introduced to their civilities by the high rank he had lately held in his country, he soon finds way to their hearts by the dignity and elegance of his demeanor, the light and beauty of his conversation, and the seductive and fascinating power of his address. The conquest was not a difficult one. Innocence is ever simple and credulous; conscious of no designs itself, it expects none in others; every door and portal of the heart are thrown open, and all who choose it, enter. Such was the state of Eden when the serpent entered its bowers. The prisoner," (Burr) "in a more engaging form, winding himself into the open and unpractised heart of Blennerhassett, found but little difficulty in changing the native character of that heart, and the objects of its affections. By degrees, he infuses into it the poison of his own ambition; he breathes into it the fire of his own courage; a daring and desperate thirst for glory; an ardour panting for all the storms and bustle and hurricane of life. In a short time, the whole man is changed; and every object of his former delights relinquished. No more he enjoys the tranquil scene; it has become flat and insipid to his taste. His books are abandoned; his retort and crucible thrown aside; his shrubbery blooms and breathes its fragrance upon the air in vain—he likes it not; his ear no longer drinks the melody of music—it longs for the trumpet's clangour and the cannon's roar. Even the prattle of his babes, once so sweet, no longer affects him, and the angel smile of his wife, who hitherto touched his bosom with ecstasy so unspeakable, is now unfelt for and unseen. Greater objects have taken possession of his soul; his imagination has been dazzled by visions of diadems, and stars, and garters, and titles of nobility;—he has been taught to burn, with restless emulation, at the names of Cromwell, Cæsar, and Bonaparte," &c.

Leaving his daughter with Mrs. Blennerhassett, Burr proceeded immediately to recruiting men for the expedition. His mind was now fully determined on the enterprise. Every thing appeared favourable, and what was to prevent the realization of his dreams?

"Far away to the south-west, a thousand miles beyond the Mississippi, lay a vast and wealthy empire, governed by tyrants whom the people hated, and defended by troops whom soldiers should despise. For years, the riches of that kingdom were the theme of travellers. Her mines were inexhaustible and had flooded Europe with gold. Her nobles enjoyed the revenues of emperors; her capitol was said to be blazoned with jewels. It was known to look down on the lake, into whose waters the unhappy Guatemozin had cast the treasures of that long line of native princes, of which he was the last. Men dreamed of that magnificent city as Alladin dreamed of his palaces, or Columbus of Cathay. Costly statues; vessels of gold and silver; jewels of untold value; troops of the fairest Indian girls for slaves; all that the eye delighted in, or the heart of man could desire, it was currently declared, would form the plunder of Mexico. A bold adventurer, commanding an army of Anglo-Saxon soldiers, could possess himself of the empire. The times were favourable to the enterprise. The priesthood throughout Mexico was disaffected, and would gladly lend its aid to any conqueror who secured its privileges; and the priesthood then, as now, exercised a paramount influence over the weak and superstitious Mexicans. America, too, was thought to be on the eve of a Spanish war, when the contemplated expedition might easily be fitted out at New Orleans. Burr saw the glittering prize, and resolved to seize it. He would conquer this gorgeous realm, and realize, in this new world, as Napoleon did in the old, a dream of romance.

"He would surround his throne with dukes and marshals, and princes of the empire. The pomp of chivalry, the splendours of the east, should be revived in this court. Realms equally rich, and even more easy of spoil, opened to the south, to whose conquest his successors, if not himself, might aspire. Perhaps nothing would check his victorious banner until he had traversed the continent, and stood on that bold and stormy promontory, where the contending waters of the Atlantic and Pacific lash around Cape Horn."*

With that eloquence of expression and power of imagination which was peculiarly his, he infused into the minds of his auditors a thirst, like his own, for the brilliant scenes of Mexico. At Marietta he had an opportunity of meeting with the militia, who were assembled for the purpose of an annual training. Being called upon for that purpose, he exercised the regiment in a few evolutions, by which he demonstrated to the doubting his superior knowledge of military tactics, and capability for commanding. A ball succeeded the training, in the evening. The congregated beauty of the surrounding neighbourhood greeted him with their smiles; while the men of rougher mould gave encouragement to his enterprise. Offers of distinction and rank, and the dazzling dreams of wealth, were arguments irresistible to the young and adven-

---

* Anonymous.

turous; and Burr soon found himself surrounded by men impatient for the expedition.

Let it not be presumed that the honest and patriotic spirits of the West for a moment contemplated treachery to their country, or meditated a wilful violation of her laws. They who had breasted the storms of adversity, in every conceivable shape; who had scaled the barriers of the Alleghanies, amid the dangers of Indian warfare; who, for many years, had stood upon the frontier of civilization, and grappled, in deadly conflict, with the enemies of their country and their race; who had pursued the savage to his wigwam and startled him from his mountain fastness; these were the men whom impartial history must pronounce incapable of a crime so base, so revolting to the mind of every patriot. But they were deceived, in their over-credulousness, in the statement of Burr, and joined the expedition, under the well-grounded belief that Jefferson favoured it; and that, in the event of war, it would be neither illegal nor contrary to the wishes of the government.

CHAPTER VI.

Preparations for the expedition commenced—Burr's visit to Chillicothe—Cincinnati—Kentucky—Alston arrives at the island—Alston with his wife and Blennerhassett visits Lexington, Ky.—Blennerhassett is introduced to Charles Fenton Mercer—Suspicious aspect of the expedition—Situation of affairs in the United States—Apprehensions of the people—Rumours—Graham appointed a secret agent of the government—Instructions—Instructions to Gen. Wilkinson—Wilkinson demands forces of the Governor of Mississippi Territory—Is refused—Despatches Burling to Mexico—Holds a conference with Governor Claiborne at New Orleans—Merchants of New Orleans convoked—Preparations at New Orleans—Blennerhassett sets out from Kentucky for home—Meets with Mr. Mercer—Conversation—Burr's designs explained—Blennerhassett is joined by Burr at the island—Burr leaves the supervision of the boats to Blennerhassett and returns to Kentucky—Is arrested—Graham arrives at Marietta—Interview with Blennerhassett—Visits the Governor of Ohio at Chillicothe—Act of the Ohio Legislature—Militia of the State called out—Anecdotes—Mercer's visit to the island—Arrival of Comfort Tyler and his men—Find Blennerhassett disheartened as to the feasibility of the enterprise.

In the month of September, 1806, Burr commenced active preparations for the contemplated expedition. Contracts for fifteen large bateaux, sufficient to convey five hundred men, and a large keel-boat for the transportation of provision, arms, ammunition, &c., also, for flour, whisky, corn-meal, and other eatables, were entered into; for the most of which Blennerhassett became responsible. Much of the corn, from which the meal was made, was raised and kiln-dried on the island.

While these operations were being carried forward, Burr visited Chillicothe, then the seat of government of Ohio, and continued his trip to Cincinnati, and thence to Kentucky. The object of this tour was to extend his acquaintance, and add new recruits to his enterprise. Each private was to supply himself with proper arms and clothing, and to receive, as a compensation for his services, one hundred acres of land on the Washita: officers were to receive according to their grade.

In the month of October, Mrs. Alston, then at the island with the family of Blennerhassett, was joined by her husband, who had fallen in with Burr's plans, and, in all probability, was to accompany him on his tour. They, in company with Blennerhassett, proceeded to Lexington, Kentucky; leaving the island and its affairs under the supervision of Mrs. Blennerhassett.

On their passage down, they met with the distinguished Charles Fenton Mercer, who was an old college-mate of Mr. Alston, at the New

Jersey College. Having been introduced to the acquaintance of Blennerhassett, Mr. Mercer remarks, that the reputation which he had acquired for talents, learning and taste, and an eccentric and somewhat romantic mode of life, rendered this interview with Blennerhassett one of the most interesting events which occurred to him during his residence on the Ohio. He, therefore, accepted with much pleasure an invitation to visit the beautiful and much celebrated island.

It was true, that, at that period, and for several weeks previous, reports were in circulation, that Blennerhassett was engaged with Burr in some common enterprise, to which many had imputed a highly criminal design. But those reports, and especially the injurious suspicions often connected with them, seemed to have arisen from pre-existing prejudices against Burr, which it was not difficult to trace to an origin very remote from the designs now ascribed to him. As the reports were believed and propagated, by those who spake of them, with a conviction and zeal proportioned to their ignorance or malignity; and as they were, in themselves, most improbable, absurd and ridiculous, Mr. Mercer considered them entitled to no consideration.

The expedition, in the eyes of many, began now to assume a serious aspect; and, through the medium of the press, attracted the attention of those more remote from the scene of preparations. Apprehension and alarm seized on the public mind, and spread dismay throughout the country. Spain had refused us compensation for her spoliations during a former war. Our commerce passing on the Mobile river continued to be obstructed by arbitrary duties and vexatious searches. The boundaries of Louisiana remained in dispute, producing much uneasiness and discontent in the south-west. The government had been deterred from a declaration of war, by Napoleon, from the effects of whose arms Europe was then trembling, and who had intimated that France would take part with Spain in any contest she might have against the United States. Added to this, the impressment of American seamen by British vessels; and our nation was at once reduced to a situation of painful humiliation.

Feeble, indeed, would be that aid which a disunited people could render, in time of perils such as these. Never before, in the history of the nation, had rebellion and disunion so openly avowed itself. How far this disaffection extended, was, to many, a matter of mysterious and anxious conjecture. Burr had, but a few years previous, closed a close and popular canvass for the Executive chair. It was known that, not only his partisans, but his personal friends, were numerous; many of whom were men of wealth and influence, who could rally to their standard a formidable number to support the cause of faction. Party malevolence and personal animosity added fuel to the flame, and ultimate ruin hung, as a withering pall, over the destinies of the country.

A rumour was gaining ground that a numerous and powerful association, extending, from New York, through the Western States, to the Gulf of Mexico, had been formed; that eight or ten thousand men were to rendezvous in New Orleans, at no distant period; and, from thence, with the cöoperation of a naval force, follow Burr to Vera Cruz; that agents from Mexico had come to Philadelphia during the summer, and had given assurances that the landing of the expedition would be followed by such an immediate and general insurrection as would insure the submission of the existing government, and silence all opposition in a very few weeks; that a part of the association would descend the Alleghany river, and the first general rendezvous would be at the rapids of the

Ohio, towards the twentieth of October, and, from thence, the aggregate force was to proceed in light-boats, with the utmost velocity, to New Orleans, under an expectation of being joined on the rout by men raised in the State of Tennessee and other quarters.

It was said that the maritime cöoperation relied on was from a British squadron in the West Indies; that active and influential characters had been engaged in making preparations for six or eight months past, which were in such a state of readiness that it was expected the van would reach New Orleans in December, where the necessary organization and equipment would be completed, with such promptitude that the expedition would leave the Mississippi towards the first of February. It was added, that the revolt of the slaves, along the river, was relied on, as an auxiliary measure; and that the seizure of the banks of New Orleans was contemplated, to supply the funds necessary to carry on the enterprise.*

Mr. Jefferson, then President of the United States, through considerations of caution, and to quell the apprehension of danger, adopted the precautionary measure of appointing Graham,

* Martin's History of Louisiana.

the Secretary of the territory of Orleans, a secret agent of the government, with instructions to spy out and investigate any plot hostile to the national interest; empowering him to enter into conferences with the civil and military authorities in the West, and, with their aid, to call on the spot whatever should become necessary to discover the designs of the supposed conspirators; and also to bring the offenders to punishment, when he should have fully ascertained their intentions.

It being known, at this time, that many boats were in preparation, stores and provisions collected, and an unusual number of suspicious characters in motion, on the Ohio and its tributaries, orders were given to the Governor of the Mississippi and Orleans Territories, and to the commanders of the land and naval forces, to be on their guard against surprise, and in constant readiness to resist any enterprise that might be attempted.

On the eighth of November, instructions had been sent to General Wilkinson, to hasten on accommodations with the Spanish commander on the Sabine, and fall back with his principal force on the hither bank of the Mississippi.*

* Jefferson's Message of 22d January, 1807.

This order, however, had been anticipated by Wilkinson, who, on the fifth of the same month, three days previous to the despatch of the instructions, having received intelligence that the Spanish camp on the Sabine would be broken up on that day, began his march towards Natchitoches. Immediately on his arrival there, he had directed Porter to proceed with the utmost expedition, and to repair, mount, and equip for service, every piece of ordnance in the city; to employ all hands in preparing shells, grape, canister and musket cartridges, with buck-shot; to have every fieldpiece ready, with horse, harness and drag-rope, and to mount six or eight battering cannons on fort St. Charles and fort St. Louis—below and above the city—and along its front, flanks and rear.

Porter left Natchitoches with all the artifices, and company of one hundred men, and had been followed by Cushing with the rest of the forces, leaving only one company behind. Wilkinson, on his way to New Orleans, stopped at Natchez, and made application to the Executive of the Mississippi Territory for a detachment of five hundred men of its militia to proceed with him; but, declining to communicate his motives, in making the requisition, the governor refused a compliance with so mysterious a demand.

From this place, Wilkinson, on the fifteenth of November, despatched Burling, one of his aids, to Mexico, for the ostensible purpose of apprising the Viceroy of the danger with which his sovereign's dominions were menaced; but, in reality, (as the general mentions in his memoirs,) on grounds of public policy and professional enterprise, to attempt to penetrate the veil which concealed the topographical rout to the city of Mexico, and the military defences which intervened—feeling that the equivocal relation of the two countries justified the *ruse*.*

As soon as Wilkinson arrived in New Orleans, he held an interview with Governor Claiborne; at which time it was deemed expedient to convoke the merchants of the city, to adopt precautionary measures for their security. The latter, in an animated address, exhorted them to assist him in his efforts for the defence of the city, and solemnly swore, in the enthusiastic style peculiar to him, that, if it were taken by the vessels, he would perish in the endeavour to repel the assault. The meeting adopted, unanimously, some spirited and patriotic resolutions. A considerable sum was subscribed to be distributed as bounty among such sailors as might engage to

* Martin's History of Louisiana.

serve on board the ships. Many of the guns of the city were placed upon the merchantmen in the river; and a respectable fleet was suddenly formed, to oppose that of the British, which was expected from the West Indies.

In the meanwhile, Blennerhassett, having received information from his wife, (who despatched to him a special messenger for that purpose,) that his affairs were in danger, and required his immediate attention, left Kentucky, about the first of October, for home. Near Point Pleasant, he again met with Mr. Mercer, at the house of Col. Andrew Lewis, a veteran in the revolutionary and various Indian wars.

In conversation, he adverted, with much sensibility, to the reports in circulation, relevant to Aaron Burr and himself, which were daily becoming more exaggerated, all of which he declared were utterly false. He was the last man in the world, he said, who would disturb the peace and impair the prosperity of the United States. Weary of political situations, in his native country, he had sought and found an asylum in America, the tranquillity of which he could never violate. He had, indeed, he admitted, united with Col. Burr, (whom public rumour had injured as much as himself,) in the plan of colonizing and improving a large tract of country, on the Red river, originally granted by the King of Spain, to Baron Bastrop, and lately purchased by Burr, of a gentleman in Kentucky. The tract contained eight hundred thousand acres; and the consideration which Col. Burr and himself were to pay for it, was forty thousand dollars; but, by distributing a part of it in hundred-acre farms, among a number of emigrants, they had no doubt, on the most moderate estimate, of being able to raise the value of the remainder to more than one million of dollars.

Shortly after his arrival at the island, Blennerhassett was joined by Burr, who had also returned from Kentucky and his journey through Ohio. He did not remain long, however, at the scene of preparations on the Muskingum. Having completed his arrangements, he left Blennerhassett to superintend the construction of the boats; to make the necessary preparation; and to follow him, as soon as practicable, to the mouth of the Cumberland, with the men, provisions and boats.

Burr proceeded down the Ohio to Kentucky, where he had hardly landed, before he was arrested, and carried before the United States' Court, on a charge of "treasonable practices, and a design to attack the Spanish domains, and thereby endanger the peace of the United States."

The arrest was premature, and Burr was discharged for want of evidence.

Near the middle of November, Graham, the government's confidential agent, proceeded to Marietta, where extensive preparations were going on. Here he met, and held an interview with Blennerhassett. After discoursing upon the subject of the expedition, with a frankness which was only warranted by a well-founded belief, (from what Burr had previously intimated,) that Graham was considered as one of the recruits, Blennerhassett read to him some communications he had just received, by the hand of Capt. Elliot, and also one from Burr, in relation to his arrest and trial at Frankfort, upon which Blennerhassett animadverted with great severity. Graham, finding Blennerhassett was labouring under a delusion, in regard to the part that he was to perform in the transaction, informed him that Burr's representations, as to him (Graham) being with or favouring the expedition, were groundless. With no little surprise, he asked Graham whether he had not heard of an association, in New Orleans, for the invasion of Mexico. Upon Graham venturing to assure him that there was no such an association there, Blennerhassett stated that he had been informed, by Bradford, the printer of the

"Gazette d'Orleans," that about three hundred men had already joined the expedition.

Considering Blennerhassett most cruelly deceived, Graham endeavoured to draw him off from the undertaking, in which he was engaged; and conceiving it the policy of the government to prevent, rather than to punish such enterprises, he informed Blennerhassett that, so far from being concerned in the plan, he was the government's authorized agent to inquire into the facts relative to the enterprise, in the western country, and to take such steps as might be necessary for repressing it. He then stated to Mr. Blennerhassett, from reasons drawn from Burr's visit to New Orleans, during the preceding summer—from the information which the government had received—and from the nature of the preparations which Blennerhassett himself was then making, *why* he believed the object of Burr was either to attack the territories of Spain or those of the United States;—and added, that any collection of armed men on the Ohio river, would, under the circumstances, be considered a violation of the laws, and repressed accordingly.

The object and extent of the preparations at Marietta having been fully ascertained, by Graham, according to instructions, he visited the Governor of Ohio, at Chillicothe, to procure the aid of the State authorities, in suppressing the suspected formidable measures. Governor Tiffin communicated the matter to the Legislature—then in session, whereupon an act was immediately passed, entitled "An Act to prevent certain acts hostile to the peace and tranquillity of the United States, within the jurisdiction of the State of Ohio."*

Under this act, Governor Tiffin ordered out the militia of the adjacent neighbourhood, under command of Major-general Buell, of Marietta, with instructions, to that officer, to take forcible possession of the boats and stores, not only upon the Muskingum, but also of all others of a suspicious character descending the Ohio.

A warlike array of undisciplined militia, with cannon, necessary equipage and arms, stationed themselves along the banks of the river, to cut off the forces expected from above. Many amusing jokes were played off at the expense of the raw recruits during this campaign;—such as setting an empty tar-barrel on fire, and placing it in an old boat or raft of logs, to float by in the darkness of the night. The sentries, after duly hailing, and receiving no answer, would fire a shot to enforce their command; but still "dread

* Chase's Statutes of Ohio, vol. i. p. 553.

silence reigned," and calmly the phantom vessel, with her stolid crew, floated onward and downward, in utter recklessness—as if the crowing of a farm-house cock only had disturbed the night's calm silence. Irritated at such manifest contempt of their high authority, they plunged into the stream to seize the boat and capture its luckless navigators; when, "confusion utterly confounded!" naught appeared but the remains of a log and a barrel, which some laughter-loving wag had freighted for their mischance and his amusement.

On another occasion, they had learned that Tyler* and his men had passed down the river as far as Blennerhassett's island, from whence he was expected to return, to recapture the boats and provisions. To cut off all possible communication with Marietta, where the boats were tied, particular instructions were given, in the evening, to bring away all the water-crafts from the lower side of the Muskingum. Several sailors, who boarded on the opposite shore, considered the opportunity for sport too favourable to pass unimproved. The plan first proposed, for the accomplishment of this end, was to raise an armed party, with blank cartridges, and fire at

---

* Comfort Tyler was one of Burr's principal captains.

the sentinels. Upon strict search, however, they found that all the muskets, blunderbusses, rifles, and shot-guns, had been previously appropriated by the militia. The cannon was then thought of, when this, also, it was ascertained, had been called to the aid of the State authorities. Determined not to be defeated, in the laugh they had promised themselves, they resorted to the expedient of emptying a half-keg of powder into a canvas sack, wrapping it closely with twine. This they deposited under ground, care being taken to leave a communication with the contents by means of a priming-hole and slow-match. At midnight, when all, save the faithful and lonely sentinels, were enjoying that repose so necessary to the refreshment of the wearied soldier, after a destructive attack

"On whisky and peach-brandy,"*

A confused and foreboding sound, from the opposite shore, grated unmusically on the ear of the guards. Although appearances were somewhat ominous, yet they concluded not to disturb the slumbers of their brothers in arms until a more satisfactory demonstration had been made. For this opportunity they were not kept long in suspense. Suddenly the earth began to heave and throe,

---

* See Appendix, No. 3.

as if drunk with the heel-taps of the soldier's glasses, and, following in quick succession, a report, that many mistook for the summoning trump of the end of time. The scene which succeeded is more easily imagined than described. Those less confused, did, indeed, take time to adjust their out-side garments, but much the greater number started with nothing but their nether vestments, without regard to uniform or military parade. Here stood one, vainly struggling to thrust his feet through the arm-holes and sleeves of his linsey *warmus*, while, at his side, a companion had drawn his pants over his shoulders, illustrating, most ludicrously, but literally, the lines of doggerel :—

"Put on his shirt outside his coat,
And tied his breeches round his throat."

Shivering, in the chill winds of December, they "hurried in hot haste" to the tanta-ran-ta of the trumpeter, and the rub-a-dub-dub of the "drum-major-general." Whether any had taken the precaution to "load" or "prime" is a question which time and reflection have never settled. The major, who was a tailor, is said to have charged the cannon with his *goose* ;—the State having made no provision for ammunition. The deputy, as he mounted his horse, was heard to say, that, "as great men were scarce, he thought it best to flee from danger." Had Tyler and his men been the real cause of their alarm, he would doubtless have met with a stern resistance, but, fortunately for him, he was unconsciously asleep at the island.*

On Saturday evening, the 6th of December, Mr. Mercer, in the course of his journey east of the mountains, stopped at the island, with the view of purchasing this "most elegant seat in Virginia." Finding, however, that Blennerhassett estimated it at fifty thousand dollars, which (he remarked) was ten thousand less than it had cost him, Mr. Mercer abandoned the idea of purchasing; and the rest of his time, during the visit, was spent in conversation with Blennerhassett and his accomplished lady. It turned upon his removal to the "Washita"—the name of his new purchase. With great earnestness, he pressed Mr. Mercer to become a participant;—suggesting how much it would augment his fortune, and enforcing the inducement by an assurance that the society he invited him to join would soon become the most agreeable and select in America. He spoke of Burr as the moral head of it; and when Mr. Mercer expressed a doubt of the per-

---

* See the description, by General Tupper, in the Appendix, No. 3.

manency and happiness of a union formed under such auspices, and dwelt upon such traits of Burr's general character as he deemed exceptionable, Blennerhassett vindicated him, with the enthusiasm of an ardent admirer.

Blennerhassett, having intended to visit Marietta on Sunday evening, Mr. Mercer proposed accompanying him, as that was directly on his route. As a tribute of merited gratitude, he remarks, that he left the mansion in perfect good will to all its inhabitants; regretting that the engagements of its proprietor and his own dreary journey, but just begun in the commencement of winter, forbade him to prolong a visit which, although so transient, had afforded him so much pleasure. All that he had seen or heard corresponded so little with the criminal designs imputed to Blennerhassett, that, if he could have visited him with unfavourable sentiments, they would have vanished before the light of a species of evidence which, if not reducible to the strictest rules of legal testimony, had, nevertheless, a potent influence over all sensitive hearts; and which, though it do not possess the formal sanction of an oath, hath often in it a great deal more truth than statements thus verified.

"What!" remarks Mr. Mercer, "will a man who, weary of the agitations of the world—of its noise and vanity, has unambitiously retired to a solitary island in the heart of a desert, and created a terrestrial paradise, the very flowers, and shrubs, and vines of which he had planted and nurtured with his own hands; a man whose soul is accustomed to toil in the depths of literature; whose ear is framed to the harmony of sound, and whose touch and breath daily awaken it from a variety of melodious instruments; will such a man start up, in the decline of life, from the pleasing dream of seven years' slumber, to carry fire and sword to the peaceful habitations of men who have never done him wrong? Are his musical instruments and his library to become the equipage of a camp? Will he expose a lovely and accomplished woman, and two little children, to whom he seems so tenderly attached, to the guilt of treason, and to the horrors of war;—a treason so desperate?—a war so unequal? Were not all his preparations better adapted to the innocent and useful purpose which he avowed, rather than to the criminal and hazardous enterprise which was imputed to him? Whence arose those imputations? From his union with Col. Burr. But, it is evident he has been led to this union from his admiration of the genius, and confidence in the virtue and honour of the person with whom it has connected him. That which, with a harsh-judging world, is the foundation of a belief of his guilt, when thoroughly and candidly examined, carries on its face, therefore, the stamp of his innocence."

On the same day of the arrival of Mr. Mercer at the island, also landed Comfort Tyler, of New York, and a small party of men under his command. He found Blennerhassett much disheartened as to the enterprise, and nearly resolved to abandon it altogether. Through the pursuasive eloquence of Mrs. Blennerhassett, however, who had now enlisted in the undertaking with her whole soul, and the arrival of Tyler's men, "the lord of the isle," as if some demon of evil haunted his footsteps, and urged him on to an unknown destiny, yielding rather to the wishes of others than to the sounder dictates of his own better judgment—again embarked his fortune and fame in the enterprise of Burr.

On the eighth of December, 1806, favoured by the darkness of the night, a company of young men from Belpré attempted, secretly, to bring away the boats and stores ready for embarkation. They had nearly succeeded, when their movements were observed by the militia, and all of the boats but one were captured. This, with its party, successfully reached the island, notwithstanding the efforts of the guards to prevent it.

CHAPTER VII.

Burr despatches Swartwout to Wilkinson—Letter—Wilkinson communicates its substance to the President—Proclamation of the President—Virginia militia called out under command of Col. Hugh Phelps—Blennerhassett escapes with Tyler and his forces down the Ohio—Phelps proceeds to the island—Finds it deserted—Ineffectual attempt to arrest Blennerhassett at Point Pleasant—Effect of the President's Proclamation trusted to for some time in the State of Tennessee—But similar instructions sent to that State also—Graham leaves Frankfort for Nashville—The movements of Burr—Kentucky militia ordered out—Burr's Flotilla—Burr leaves the Cumberland—Lands at Fort Massac—Is visited by the commander, Captain Bissell—Supplies Burr with a messenger to convey a letter to the Lead Mines in Missouri—His wife presents Burr with provisions—Burr and his party proceed to Chickasaw Bluffs—Has an interview with the commander, Lieutenant Jacob Jackson—Fails in his designs—Communication of the President to Wilkinson—Burr supplies himself with lead, tomahawks, &c., and proceeds to Palmyra, and thence to Bayou Pierre.

On the twenty-ninth of July, 1806, Burr had despatched, by the hands of Swartwout, to Gen. Wilkinson, the following communication, in *cypher*, from Philadelphia.

"I have obtained funds and have actually commenced the enterprise . . . . detachments from different points, and under different pretences, will rendezvous on the Ohio, 1st Nov. Every thing, internal and external favours views. Protection of England is secured. T—— is going to Jamaica to arrange with the admiral on that station: it will meet on the Mississippi. England . . . . navy of the United States are ready to join, and final orders are given to my friends and followers . . . . it will be a host of choice spirits . . . . Wilkinson shall be second to Burr only.—Wilkinson shall dictate the rank and promotions of his officers.—*Burr* will proceed westward, 1st August . . . . never to return . . . . with him go his daughter . . . . the husband will follow, in October, with a *corps* of worthies, and . . . . send forth . . . . with an intelligent and confidential friend, with whom Burr may confer. He shall return immediately, with further interesting details—this is essential to concert and harmony of movement. Send a list of all persons known to Wilkinson west of the mountains, who may be useful, with a note delineating their character. By your messenger, send me four or five of the commissions of your officers, which you can borrow under any pretence you please.—They shall be returned faithfully. Already are orders given to the contractor to forward six months' provision to points Wilkinson may name; this shall not be used until the last moment, and then under proper injunctions; the project is brought to a point so long desired. Burr guarantees the result with his life and honour—with the lives, and honour, and the fortunes of hundreds, the best blood of our country. Burr's plan of operation is to move down rapidly, from the falls, on the 15th of November, with the first five hundred or one thousand men, in light boats now constructing for that purpose, to be at Natchez between the 5th and 15th of December—there to meet Wilkinson—there to determine whether it will be expedient, in the first instance, to seize on, or pass by, Baton Rouge.... on receipt of this, send Burr an answer,.... draw on Burr for all expenses, &c. The people of the country to which we are going are prepared to receive us; their agents, now with Burr, say that if we will protect their religion, and will not subject them to a foreign power, that, in three weeks, all will be settled. The gods invite to glory and fortune—it remains to be seen whether we deserve the boon. The bearer of this goes express to you; he will hand a formal letter of introduction to you, from Burr, he is a man of inviolable honour and perfect discretion, formed to execute rather than project—capable of relating facts with fidelity, and incapable of relating them otherwise. He is thoroughly informed of the plans and intentions of —— and will disclose to you, as far as you inquire and no farther; he has imbibed a reverence for your character, and may be embarrassed in your presence; put him at ease, and he will satisfy you."

Wilkinson, having received this despatch some time in November, communicated its substance to the President, who, on the twenty-seventh of the same month issued the following

Proclamation.

Whereas, information has been received, that sundry persons, citizens of the United States or residents within the same, are conspiring and confederating together, to begin and set on foot, provide and prepare, the means for a military expedition, or enterprise, against the dominions of Spain; that, for this purpose, they are fitting out and arming vessels, in the Western waters of the United States; collecting provisions, arms, military stores and other means; are deceiving and seducing honest and well-meaning citizens, under various pretences, to engage in their criminal enterprises; are organizing officers, and arming themselves, for the same, contrary to the laws in such case made and provided:—I have thought fit, therefore, to issue this my *proclamation*, warning and enjoining all faithful citizens, who have been led, without due knowledge or consideration, to participate in the said unlawful enterprises, to withdraw from the same without delay: and commanding all persons whatsoever, engaged or concerned in the same, to cease all further proceedings therein, as they will answer the contrary at their peril, and incur prosecution with all the rigours of the law. And I hereby enjoin and require all officers, civil and military, of the United States or of any of the States or territories, and especially all governors and other executive authorities; all judges, justices and other officers of the peace; all military officers of the army and navy of the United States, and officers of the militia; to be vigilant, each within his respective department, and according to his functions, in searching out and bringing to condign punishment, all persons engaged or concerned in such enterprise, in seizing and retaining, subject to the disposition of the law, all vessels, arms, military stores or other means, provided or providing for the same, and, in general, in preventing the carrying on such expedition or enterprise, by all the lawful means within their power; and I require all good and faithful citizens, and others, within the United States, to be aiding and assisting herein, and especially in the discovery, apprehension and bringing to justice of all such offenders, in preventing the execution of their unlawful designs, and in giving information against them to the proper authorities.

In testimony, &c.

THOMAS JEFFERSON.

By the President:

JAMES MADISON,
Secretary of State.

Under the authority, and by virtue of this proclamation, the Virginia militia, of Wood county, were called out, by command of Col. Hugh Phelps, of Parkersburg,* as soon as he had received intelligence of the same, which was not until the eighth or ninth of December.

On the tenth of the month, Blennerhassett, having received information of the preparations making by Col. Phelps, (who, it was expected, would march to the island on the following day,) to take possession of his person, boats, and stores, departed, under cover of night, with Tyler and his forces, leaving Mrs. Blennerhassett, with the two little boys, to follow.

In thus abandoning the tender partner of his bosom, and those lesser lights of his affectionate regard, Blennerhassett had not mistaken the

* A town in Virginia, two miles above Blennerhassett's island.

character of the individual who, he rightly presumed, was soon to take charge of his mansion. From intimate association with the man, he knew that innocence and feebleness would ever be sacredly regarded by Col. Phelps; that, while duty to the calls of his country compelled him to exercise the functions of his office, and that, too, in defeating the plans of his most intimate friend and associate, that power would be exerted with the strictest adherence to the laws of humanity and the highest sentiments of honour; that while no menaces would deter him from the disagreeable duty imposed, no act of wanton violence should stain the honour of the friend.

On the succeeding morning, Col. Phelps, with a small body of men, proceeded to the island. They found it deserted by its proprietor. Inquiries were made, among the servants, who informed them of the circumstances of the preceding evening; adding, that Mrs. Blennerhassett was then on her way to Marietta, to secure, if possible, the boat originally constructed for the conveyance of Blennerhassett and his family to the Washita.

Leaving the greater portion of his men in possession of the premises, Col: Phelps started across the country to intercept the descending boats, at the mouth of the Great Kanawha. None having passed, during the previous day, answering to the description of those of which he was in pursuit, Col. Phelps informed the citizens of his designs, and procured a party to watch the river that night. Accordingly, a large fire was built upon the bank of the river, around which the watch attempted to keep their midnight vigils. Following that ancient custom of "keeping the spirits up by pouring spirits down"—like the model "officer," who was enamoured of the "landlady of France"—their revels propitiated the sleepy god, and a sweet forgetfulness of earthly cares and earthly duties soon gave evidence of quiet consciences. Taking advantage of the darkness of the night, Blennerhassett glided silently by, without disturbing the slumbers of the guard, and, before the early dawn, was many miles beyond his discomfited pursuers. At the mouth of the Cumberland, he joined the flotilla of Burr, which was then awaiting accessions both from that and the Ohio river.

Not apprized, till late, that boats were being constructed on the Cumberland, the effect of the President's proclamation had been trusted to, for some time, in the State of Tennessee; but, on the 19th of December, similar communications and instructions with those of the neighbouring

States, were despatched, by express, to the governor, and a general officer of the western division of the State; and, on the 23d, Graham, the agent, left Frankfort for Nashville, to put into activity the means of that State also. Burr, however, had been too prompt, in his movements, for the agents of the government. On the 22d of the same month, he had descended the Cumberland, with two boats, laden with provision and a few additional forces.

The Governor of Kentucky, after the arrest and discharge of Burr, hearing of his arrival at the mouth of the Cumberland, with a flotilla of numerous vessels; and that he was there congregating his forces, ordered out the militia for his arrest, but Burr, anticipating the movement, slipped his moorings, and proceeded further down the river.

The flotilla now consisted of four boats under command of Tyler, two under Burr, two under Floyd, one under Ellis, one under Blennerhassett, and a commissary boat, under Dean.

On the evening of the twenty-ninth, Burr stopped a short distance below Fort Massac, then under the command of Capt. Bissell. The following morning, he was visited, at his boats, by that officer, who gave him a polite invitation to visit the fort and partake of its hospitalities. It is due to Capt. Bissell to state, (although the evidence on this point is conflicting,) that he was, at that time, without any instructions from the government. He remarks, that he had learned, unofficially, of Burr's arrest and acquittal in Kentucky; hence, he concluded, that his mission was one of peace, and for the purpose, ostensibly held out, "of colonizing the Bastrop lands." He furnished Burr with a messenger, to convey a communication to the lead mines in Missouri, as well as one or two men for his enterprise, and a small quantity of provision; the latter, however, Bissell asserts, was sent by his wife, who was an early acquaintance of Burr, and who returned it, in compliment for a barrel of apples, which Burr had forwarded to her.

On the evening of the third of January, 1807, Burr, with one boat, landed at Chickasaw Bluffs, a military station at that time commanded by Lieut. Jacob Jackson. He immediately despatched a messenger to the commander of the fort, to inquire if quarters could be furnished him during the night, who shortly returned with an affirmative answer. The following morning, he had an interview with Jackson, on the subject of the expedition, in which he stated that he was going on a project of which many wished to know, but, from their inquisitiveness, he was not disposed to gratify them, but assured him that it was an enterprise which would be honourable to him, (Jackson,) and would be the making of those who should follow him, provided they survived the undertaking. Every argument was resorted to, to shake the fidelity of that young officer to his country, and prevail on him to join the expedition, with the whole of the forces under his command. To the ardent and enthusiastic mind of youth, panting for scenes of glory and distinction, his offers of fame and emolument were truly tempting; particularly as they were enforced by the sophistical reasoning of that astute and experienced diplomatist. But, to his honour, and to the honour of American youths—particularly to American officers—he foiled the attempts of the seducer, and came off moral victor in the attack. While in the service of his country, no offer of wealth, or place, or power, could decoy him from the path of rectitude. The government had confided the command of that fort to his youthful hands, and so long as he retained that trust, his best energies should be exerted to preserve it with fidelity and honour.

On the third of January, 1807, the President despatched the following communication to Gen. Wilkinson:—"I had yesterday intended to recommend, to Gen. Dearborn, the writing to you, weekly, by post, to convey information of our affairs, in the west, as long as they are interesting; because it is possible, though not probable, you might sometimes get the information quicker, this way, than down the river; but the general received, yesterday, information of the death of his son, in the East Indies, and, of course, cannot now attend to business. I therefore, write you a hasty line, for the present week, and send it, in duplicate, by the Athens and Nashville route.

"The information, in the enclosed paper, as to proceedings in the State of Ohio, is correct. Blennerhassett's flotilla, of fifteen boats and two hundred barrels of provisions, is seized, and there can be no doubt that Tyler's flotilla is also taken; because, on the 17th December, we know there was a sufficient force assembled at Cincinnati, to intercept it there, and another party was in pursuit of it on the river above. We are assured that these two flotillas composed the whole of the boats provided. Blennerhassett and Tyler had fled down the river. I do not believe that the number of persons engaged for Burr has ever amounted to five hundred; though some have carried them to one thousand or fifteen hundred. A part of these were engaged as settlers of Bastrop's land, but the greater part were engaged under the express assurance that the projected enterprise was against Mexico, and secretly authorized by this government. Many expressly enlisted in the name of the United States. The proclamation, which reached Pittsburgh, December second, and other parts of the river successively, undeceived both these classes; and, of course, drew them off; and I have never seen any proof of their having assembled more than forty men, in two boats, from Beaver, fifty in Tyler's flotilla, and the boatmen of Blennerhassett. I believe, therefore, that the enterprise may be considered as crushed; but we are not to relax, in our attentions, until we hear what has passed at Louisville. If every thing, from that place upwards, be successfully arrested, there is nothing from below that [is] to be feared. Be assured that Tennessee, and, particularly, General Jackson, are faithful. The orders lodged at Massac and the Chickasaw Bluffs will probably secure the interception of such fugitives from justice as may escape at Louisville; so that I think you will never see one of them. Still, I would not wish, till we hear from Louisville, that this information should relax your preparations in the least, except as far as to dispense with the militia of Mississippi and Orleans, leaving their homes, under our orders of November twenty-fifth. Only let them consider themselves under requisition; and be in a state of readiness, should any force, too great for your regulars, escape down the river. You will have been sensible that those orders were given while we supposed you were on the Sabine, and the supposed crisis did not admit the formality of their being passed by you. We considered Fort Adams as the place to make a stand, because it covered the mouth of Red River. You have preferred New Orleans, on the apprehension of a fleet from the West Indies. Be assured, there is not any foundation for such an expectation; but the lying exaggerations of these traitors to impose on others and swell their pretended means. The very man whom they reported to you as having gone to Jamaica and to bring the fleet, has never been from home, and has regularly communicated to me every thing which had passed between Burr and him. France or Spain would not send a fleet to take Vera Cruz; and, though one of the expeditions, now near arriving from England, is probably for Vera Cruz, and perhaps already there, yet the state of things between us renders it impossible they should countenance an enterprise unauthorized by us. Still, I repeat, that these grounds of security must not stop our proceedings or preparations until they are further confirmed. Go on, therefore, with your works for the defence of New Orleans, because they will always be useful, only looking to what should be permanent rather than means merely temporary. You may expect further information as we receive it; and, though I expect it will be such as will place us at our ease, yet we must not place ourselves so, until we be certain, but act on the possibility that the resources of our enemy may be greater and deeper than we are yet informed.

"Your two confidential messengers delivered their charges safely. One arrived yesterday, only, with your letter of November 12th. The oral communications he made me are truly important. I beseech you, take the most special care of the two letters which he mentioned to me—the one in cipher, the other from another conspirator of high standing—and send them to me by the first conveyance you can trust. It is necessary that all important testimony should be brought to one centre, in order that the guilty may be convicted and the innocent left untroubled."

On the fifth of January, having supplied himself with thirty pounds of lead and three dozen tomahawks, together with other articles, Burr proceeded down to Palmyra, and thence to Bayou Pierre.

CHAPTER VIII.

Morgan Neville, and William Robinson, Junior—Embark from Pittsburgh in a flat-boat—Espied by the Wood county militia and arrested—Escorted to the island to await the return of Col. Phelps—Difficulties with the militia—Trial of the young men—Conduct of the militia on the island—Mrs. Blennerhassett's return from Marietta—Her fortitude on the occasion—Embarrassed situation—Accepts the offer of the young men to convey her to her husband—Col. Phelps's return to the island—Young men embarrassed at the announcement of his arrival—Character and description of Col. Phelps—Rebukes the militia for their riotous conduct—His politeness to the young men—Proffers his services in accelerating Mrs. Blennerhassett's arrangement to go to her husband—Apologizes for the misbehaviour of his men—Mrs. Blennerhassett prepares to depart—Leaves the island in company with the young men—Passes the mouth of the Cumberland—Disappointed in not finding her husband—Arrives at Bayou Pierre, and is restored to Blennerhassett—Painful situation of Burr and Blennerhassett—Burr sinks the arms, for the expedition, in the Mississippi.

Morgan Neville and William Robinson, jun., with a party of fourteen young men, early in December, embarked, from Pittsburgh, in a flat-boat. Most of these were sons of gentlemen of affluence and ease, who knew but little of the realities of life, further than was learned within the walls of an academy.

They had proceeded down the river, as far as Parkersburg, when their boat having been driven on the shore, by the ice, during the night, they were espied by the Wood county militia, and the whole party arrested as accomplices of Burr.

With "savage magnificence," they were escorted to the island, to await the return of Col. Phelps, who was then absent, at Point Pleasant, in an ineffectual attempt to arrest Blennerhassett. Somewhat chagrined at their luckless adventure, so far, the young men endeavoured to pass their time as pleasantly as possible, by ridiculing the militia, and threatening them with the strong arm of the law.

But the intrepid captors were not to be deterred from duty. They parried the sarcasm of their adversaries, and occasionally retorted with considerable effect. The impertinence of the captives, at length, becoming insupportable, three justices of the peace were sent for, to institute an examination into the facts—to commit, for further trial, or acquit, the young men, as the evidence might warrant.

They were accordingly arraigned, and, after a full investigation of the facts, mostly upon the evidence of the young men themselves, the court acquitted them of all hostile designs against the United States.

"During the trial, the mob spirit of the militia began to run riot, and, by the time it was ended, all was confusion. The well-stored cellars of the mansion began to pour forth their riches; drunkenness ensued; fences were torn down, to pile upon the blazing fire of the sentinels; the shrubbery was trampled under foot."

In the midst of this scene of confusion, Mrs. Blennerhassett returned, from her unsuccessful visit to Marietta, to which she had gone to procure the family boat of Blennerhassett. A scene of such desolation, and ruin of all that was fair and beautiful, and around which her young affections had clung with fond associations, was calculated to crush a heart whose native character was remarkable for its strong attachments to the objects of its love; but she had long since resigned her beautiful abode, for the more tempting lands, which her imagination had dressed in fancy's brightest colours, where serener skies and gayer flowers "shed their mingled delights" over the perennial green of nature's bosom. The successful issue of the expedition was, to her, a matter of weightier moment than all other considerations; and, thus it was, she remained unmoved amid the general wreck of her fair possessions, by the ruthless mob.

Her situation, however, was one of painful

embarrassment. Blennerhassett, having departed in haste, without making arrangements for her voyage, and the refusal of the authorities, at Marietta, to deliver her the boat, constructed for that especial purpose, left her, for a time, in almost hopeless despair of joining her husband, at the appointed place. The weather had been intensely cold, and the fast accumulating ice, in the Ohio, appeared to forbid a reunion with Blennerhassett until the following spring, when, in all probability, she could only find him in the Spanish dominions. It was, therefore, with feelings of mingled gratitude and pleasure, that she accepted the proffer of a room, in the boat of the young men, who promised to make the accommodations as comfortable, to herself and children, as the circumstances of her situation would permit.

During the course of the evening, Col. Phelps returned from his tour across the country. In this unexpected arrival, the young men had new cause of anxiety and alarm. They had congratulated themselves upon their successful defeat of the functionaries of the law, which they attributed mainly to their superior tact in mystifying their judges, and intimidating their accusers; but here was one who could not be duped by sophistical reasoning, or swerved from his duty by the fear of consequences. Although dressed in the usual style of the backwoodsmen of that day, the careless manner in which he wore his garb added gracefulness to a form both attracting and commanding. They recognised in him, an individual of physical as well as intellectual superiority, and, therefore, wisely concluded to assume a different bearing from that they before had observed towards their captors and judges.*

In a thoughtful and classic attitude, he surveyed the destruction of the premises, and the evident marks of bacchanalian revelry with which the party under his command had disgraced themselves; then, turning upon them a look of withering rebuke, he spoke in such terms of indignation as caused them to shrink with

---

* The following anecdote of him, related by General Cass, in his work styled "France, its King, Court and Government," is perfectly characteristic. He says:—

"I recollect a similar incident, which took place in a small village upon the banks of the Ohio. The Court was in session, and the presiding officer was a Colonel P———, a man of great resolution, and of herculean frame. A person entered the Court *cabin*, and, by his noise, put a stop to the proceedings. He was ordered out, and the sheriff attempted to remove him; but he put himself upon his *reserved rights*, and made such a vigorous resistance that the officer retired from the contest. Colonel P———, thereupon, descended from the bench, coolly took off his coat, gave the brawler a severe beating, and, after putting him out of the house, resumed his garment and his seat, and continued his judicial functions."

fear and trepidation. "Shame! men," he exclaimed, "shame on such conduct! You have disgraced your district, and the cause in which you are concerned!"

To the party of strangers, however, he was courteous and attentive. They soon ascertained that they had no cause to apprehend the frustration of their plans, by Colonel Phelps; indeed, so far from that, he willingly acceded to their wishes, in permitting the departure of Mrs. Blennerhassett, and proffered his services, in accelerating her arrangements to go to her husband, who, he said, he knew could never return to her. To Mrs. Blennerhassett, he expressed his deep sense of mortification, for the riotous acts of his misguided men, and assured her, of what she was already aware, had he been present the shameful act would not have occurred.

"Early next morning, Mrs. Blennerhassett commenced her preparations for a final farewell of the island Eden, where, for eight years, she had been the presiding genius. Her energy and zeal were such, that, in a few hours, she took possession of the humble chamber prepared for her in the boat, and, by the assistance of Colonel Phelps, who rivalled the young men in courtesy, the necessary stores and furniture were embarked. On the seventeenth day of December, the boat swung from the shore, lashed to another of the same class, belonging to A. W. Putnam, of Belpré."

In the latter part of December, they passed the mouth of the Cumberland, where, it was expected she would join her husband; but, as we before have shown, he had passed out of the Ohio, into the waters of the rapid Mississippi, and moored at the entrance of Bayou Pierre. Early in January, she was restored, with her children, to Blennerhassett, who received them with that deep-felt affection which a parent and husband can only appreciate.

The situation of Burr and Blennerhassett had now become one of painful anxiety. It was evident, from surrounding circumstances, that the strong hands of the general and State governments had became too powerful for the small forces under their command. Burr saw that he was the "victim of bad faith." Those who had favoured the enterprise, at first, and gave him to understand that their aid could be relied on, abandoned their designs, upon the issuing of the President's proclamation. The authorities of the States and Territories bordering on the Ohio and Mississippi rivers had ordered out the militia, for the apprehension of the parties; and, from Pittsburgh to the Gulf, the most rigid measures had been adopted, to give an effectual check to the further progress of the expedition.

As for Blennerhassett, his situation was cheerless in the extreme. For Burr, had he abandoned his home with all its endearments—his books—his studies, his property, and, withal, was deeply involved, for debts contracted for the enterprise. As if the furies were not yet satiated, in their revenge, he was hunted and pursued, as a malefactor, and momentarily expected the chilling touch of the officer of the law, to summon him to justice.

On a dark and dreary night, in the month of January, as the flotilla pushed slowly from the landing at Petit Gulf, might have been observed the master-spirit of the expedition, seated on a rough stool, in the inclement cabin of a flat-boat, lighted only by the cheerless rays of a solitary candle, and the decaying embers of a rudely-constructed fire-place. With his face buried in his hands, while his elbows rested on a table of unplaned boards, he who had heretofore braved the disappointments which had attended his undertaking, with a fortitude that astonished, while it gave confidence to his followers, now sat gloomy and dejected. Upon what he mused is beyond the ken of human prescience; but, starting suddenly from his revery, he caught up an axe, and directed his attendant to make an opening in the side of the boat. Through this, in the silence of the night, when he supposed there was none to witness, the chests of arms for the expedition were silently sunk beneath the waters of the Mississippi.

CHAPTER IX.

Proclamation of Cowles Mead acting as Governor of the Mississippi Territory—Burr's reply—The boats are visited by George Poindexter, Attorney-General for the Territory—Object of the visit—A letter from the acting Governor—Burr's avowals—Poindexter requests his peaceable surrender—Burr declares his willingness—An interview with the acting Governor the next day is agreed upon—Terms of the agreement—Burr accordingly surrenders himself—Terms of his final surrender—He is conveyed to the town of Washington—Examination before Judge Rodney—Poindexter called on for his opinion—It is given—Judge Rodney dissents—A grand jury is required to be summoned to an adjourned session of the Supreme Court of the Mississippi Territory—Grand jury assembled—Motion to discharge—Overruled—Presentments by the grand jury—Acquitting Burr—Present the calling out of the militia of the Territory as a grievance—Also late military arrests—Astonishment of the Attorney-General—Leaves the court room—Judge Rodney displeased—Burr asks to be discharged from his recognisance—Is refused—Disguises himself and escapes—Reward offered—Suspicious circumstance—Burr's men are placed under guard—Arrests at Fort Adams and New Orleans—Conduct of Wilkinson—Treatment of General Adair—Attempt to suspend the writ of "Habeas Corpus"—Wilkinson's contempt of the writs of Habeas Corpus—Judge Workman's recommendation to the Governor—Workman becomes dissatisfied with the Governor—Resigns his office—Return of Burling from Mexico—Object of his visit—Reception of Burling by the Viceroy of Mexico—Leaves Mexico in haste—Lieutenant Swan returns from Jamaica with letter from Admiral Drake—Conveyance of prisoners to Washington and Baltimore—Their discharge.

Cowles Mead, Secretary of the Mississippi Territory, performing the duties of governor, had, on the third day of December, 1806, issued his proclamation for the arrest of "the Burr conspirators;" and, at the same time, calling on the officers of the government to take the oath of fidelity to the United States. To this proclamation, Burr, on the twelfth of January, 1807, replied in a letter of some length, in which he disavowed any designs hostile to the tranquillity of the country, stating that his only object was a peaceable settlement of the lands of his new purchase. "If the alarm which has been excited," he remarks, "should not be appeased by this declaration, I invite my fellow-citizens to visit me at this place, (Bayou Pierre,) and to receive from me, in person, such further explanations as may be necessary to their satisfaction, presuming that when my views are understood, they will receive the countenance of all good men." This letter, he requested, might be read to the militia, who, he understood, were assembled for his arrest.

Having moved his boats to the western margin of the Mississippi river, a short distance below Bayou Pierre, he was visited by George Poindexter, Esq., the Attorney-general of the Territory, who had been appointed by Mead as an honorary aid-de-camp for the arrest of the parties. The object of this visit was to gain correct information as to the situation of Burr; to ascertain his views, so far as they might be communicated; and to procure his peaceful surrender to the civil authorities.

Major Shields, who accompanied Poindexter, delivered to Burr a letter from the acting governor. In it was a sentence relating to the restoration of tranquillity in the territory, which sentence Burr repeated with a sneer; adding that he had no intention to injure the citizens of the United States. "As to any projects or plans," he continued, "which may have been formed between General Wilkinson and myself, heretofore, they are now completely frustrated by the perfidious conduct of Wilkinson; and the world must pronounce him a perfidious villain. If I am sacrificed, my portfolio will prove him to be such." He stated further, that, so far from having any designs hostile to the citizens of the United States, he intended to have met Mr. Mead, at Port Gibson, on the day of the general muster, which happened at that place about the time of his arrival at Bayou Pierre; but was deterred from so doing, by the belief that he would be assassinated, if seen passing through the territory.

Mr. Poindexter then requested him to surrender himself, peaceably, to the civil authorities;

stating that, unless he did, the governor would certainly arrest him by force. Burr declared his willingness, at all times, to submit, and proposed that an interview should take place, between himself and the acting governor, at some convenient place, on the next day; claiming protection from personal violence in the mean time.

Stipulations were entered into, by which it was agreed that Burr should be returned to his boats, if Mead should not accept of his surrender; that his flotilla should remain in the position it then occupied, until after the proposed interview should have taken place; and that, in the meanwhile, his men should commit no breach of the peace, or violate any law of the United States or Mississippi territory. The place designated for the conference was the house of Thomas Calvert, a respectable citizen of the Territory who resided near the mouth of Coles Creek, where the detachment of militia which descended the river was stationed.

Burr, accordingly, on the seventeenth day of January, dropped down the river as far as Thomas Calvert's, accompanied by Col. Fitzpatrick, who directed him to be taken in charge by Captain Davidson's company of dragoons. Here he was joined, according to appointment, by Mead; when further stipulations were required as to the terms of his surrender. These were, *first,* that the agreement entered into, for the purpose of procuring that interview, should be declared void. *Secondly,* that Burr should give himself up, unconditionally, to the civil authority. And, *thirdly,* that his boats should be searched, and all military stores and apparatus found on board, be disposed of, as the Executive should think fit.

To these terms, the acting governor required Burr's unequivocal reply, in *fifteen minutes;* and, if not agreed to, he was to be instantly returned to his boats, and the militia ordered to seize the whole party, by force.

As there was no chance of escape, the conditions were accepted of and carried into effect. Burr declared his unwillingness to fall into the hands of Wilkinson, and requested, if any attempt should be made to arrest him by a military force from New Orleans, that it might be opposed. He was conducted to the town of Washington, where he was delivered over to the custody of the law, and the examination of the witnesses immediately commenced before Judge Rodney.

Mr. Poindexter was called on, in his official capacity, as attorney-general, to give his written opinion as to the course which ought to be pursued. He, accordingly, furnished an able argument against any attempt to try the accused in the courts of the territory. He stated that they had no evidence to convict him of any offence committed in Mississippi; that the Supreme Court of the territory, to which a jury was about to be summoned, had no original jurisdiction of any prosecution, and could only take cognisance of law reserved at the trial in the Circuit Court. It was his opinion, therefore, that Burr should be sent to the city of Washington, where the Supreme Court of the United States would be in session; and the judges, attending from every part of the Union, could direct him to be tried in the District, where, from the evidence, it might appear that an overt act of treason had been committed.

But Judge Rodney thought differently; and a *venire facias* was issued, requiring the attendance of seventy-six jurors, at an adjourned session of the Supreme Court of the Mississippi Territory, to be held in February. From the number attending, at the appointed time, a grand jury of twenty-three persons was selected, who received a charge from the judge and were adjourned until the next day.

The following morning, a motion was made, by the attorney-general, to discharge the grand jury:—*first*, because the court did not possess original jurisdiction in any case. *Secondly*, because the depositions, submitted to his inspection, did not furnish sufficient evidence, to convict Burr of the offences with which he was charged, so as to bring them within the Mississippi territory; and, *thirdly*, that a warrant might issue, transmitting the accused to a court having competent jurisdiction, to try and punish him, if guilty of the crime alleged against him. The court being divided on this motion, it was, in consequence, overruled, and the grand jury retired. The attorney-general, thereupon, determined to prefer no indictment, and left the courtroom.

In the afternoon the jury returned with the following presentments:—

"The grand jury of the Mississippi Territory, on a due investigation of the evidence brought before them, are of opinion that Aaron Burr has not been guilty of any crime or misdemeanor against the laws of the United States, or of this Territory: or given any just cause of alarm or inquietude to the good people of the same.

"The grand jurors present, as a grievance, the late military expedition, unnecessarily, as they conceive, fitted out against the person and property of the said Aaron Burr, when no resistance had been made to the civil authorities.

"The grand jurors also present, as a grievance, destructive of personal liberty, the late military arrests,* made without warrant, and, as they conceive, without other lawful authority; and they do sincerely regret that so much cause has been given to the enemies of our glorious Constitution, to rejoice at such measures being adopted, in a neighbouring territory, as, if sanctioned by the Executive of our country, must sap the vitals of our political existence, and crumble this glorious fabric in the dust."

The attorney-general declared his astonishment at such unwarrantable presentments by the grand jury, and, informing the Court that he should take no notice of them, retired. Judge Rodney strongly reprobated such conduct on the part of the jury, and, after rating them in no very mild terms, dismissed them without day.

In the evening of the day on which the court sat, Burr visited the house of Colonel Osborne. He had asked to be discharged from his recognisance; as he had fully complied with its terms; but, learning that it was the intention of Gov. Williams to seize on his person the moment he was discharged by judicial authority, he requested John Dana, one of his force from Belpré, with two others, to convey him, in a boat, to a

---

* The arrests of Bollman, Swartwout, Ogden and others, at New Orleans, on suspicion of being engaged in the expedition.

point about twenty miles from Bayou Pierre, whence he could escape across the country.

Procuring a boatman's dress, in which to disguise himself, he proceeded on his tour. Upon hearing of his escape, Williams issued a proclamation, offering two thousand dollars for his apprehension and safe delivery to the proper authorities. A few days afterwards, a negro boy was discovered near the mouth of Cole's Creek, opposite which the boats were stationed, riding on a horse which belonged to Burr, and having on his surtout coat. These circumstances created a suspicion; the boy was searched, and, sewed up in the cape of his coat, was found a note to the following effect:—

"If you are yet together, keep so, and I will join you to-morrow night. In the meanwhile, put all your arms in perfect order. Ask no questions of the bearer, but tell him all you may think I wish to know. He does not know that this is from me, nor where I am."

To C. T. and D. F.*

In consequence of this discovery, Burr's men were arrested and placed under guard, where they were detained until the alarm was over.

---

* Comfort Tyler and Davis Floyd.

Many, if not all of them were permitted, occasionally, to walk about, free of restraint, on their parole of honour.

In the meanwhile, several arrests of the supposed accomplices of Burr had been made at Fort Adams and New Orleans. Among the number were Bollman, Ogden, Swartwout, Adair, Dayton, Smith and Alexander, against whom the most rigid and unjustifiable authority had been exercised, by General Wilkinson; in many cases upon bare suspicion, and without resistance, at any time, to civil authority. General Adair, who had arrived at New Orleans on the tenth of January, was besieged by one hundred and twenty men, under command of Lieutenant-colonel Kingsbury, accompanied by one of Wilkinson's aids. They seized upon him while at dinner, in a public house, dragged him from the table, and conducted him to head-quarters, where he was placed in confinement, and secreted, until an opportunity offered to convey him away.* It

---

* An Irish gentleman of wit and humour, happened to be confined in prison for debt, when it was announced to him, by one of the officials, that Gen. Adair was in the adjoining room. He immediately struck up, in a full, musical voice, to the tune of Robin Adair:

"Ye are welcome to Orleans,
Johnny Adair,—
Ye are welcome to Orleans,
Johnny Adair!

was even attempted, in the legislature of Louisiana, at the suggestion of the governor, to suspend the writ of *habeas corpus*—that inestimable guarantee to the liberties of every American citizen, more effectually to aid the harsher application of military law and military dictation.

Towards the writs of *habeas corpus*, issued by the courts, to bring the accused parties before them, Wilkinson observed the most profound contempt. So ineffectual was the process of the courts, in bringing either the prisoners or Wilkinson before them, that Judge Workman recommended to the governor, that Wilkinson should be opposed by force of arms. He stated that the violent measures of that officer had produced great discontent, alarm and agitation, in the public mind; and unless such proceedings were effectually opposed, all confidence in government would be at an end. He urged the governor to revoke the order, by which he had placed the Orleans volunteers under Wilkinson's command, and to call out and arm the rest of the militia as soon as possible. He stated it as his opinion, that an army would not oppose the civil power,

---

How does little Aaron do ?—
And Irish Blanny, too ?—
Why did'nt they come with you,
Johnny Adair ?' "

when constitutionally brought forth, or that if they did, the governor might soon have men enough to render the opposition ineffectual.*

No satisfactory answer having been made to Workman, by the governor, he again addressed him on the subject. It was notorious, he remarked, that the commander-in-chief of the military forces had, by his own authority, arrested several citizens for civil offences, and avowed on record, that he had adopted means to send them out of the Territory, openly declaring his determination to usurp the functions of the judiciary, by making himself the only judge of the guilt of the persons he suspected, and asserting, in the same manner, and without contradiction, that his measures were taken after several consultations with the governor.

Although a common case would not require the step he was taking, yet, he deemed it his duty, before any decisive measure was pursued against him, who had all the regular force, and, in pursuance of the governor's public orders, a great part of the Territory at his disposal, to ask whether the Executive had the ability to enforce the decrees of the court of the county; and if he had, whether he would deem it expedient to do

* Martin's History of Louisiana.

it in the present instance; or whether the allegations, by which Wilkinson supported the violent measures, were well founded.

"Not only the conduct and power of Wilkinson," he continued, "but various other circumstances peculiar to our present situation; the alarm excited in the public mind; the description and character of a large part of the population of the country, might render it dangerous, in the highest degree, to adopt the measure, usual in ordinary cases, of calling to the aid of the sheriff the *posse comitatus,* unless it was done with the assurance of being supported by the governor in an efficient manner."

The letter concluded, by requesting a precise and speedy answer to the preceding inquiries; and an assurance that if certain of the governor's support, the judge would forthwith punish, as the law directed, the contempt offered to the court. On the other hand, should the governor think it impracticable to afford the required aid, the court and its officers would no longer remain exposed to the contempt or insults of a man whom they were unable to punish or resist.

The same silence and indifference having been observed by the governor towards the last, as towards his former communication, Workman resigned his office as he had before indicated.*

Burling, who had been sent to Mexico, returned, without having accomplished the object of his mission. It appears that, instead of his being sent "to penetrate the veil which concealed the topographical route to the city of Mexico, and the military defences which intervened," as alleged by Wilkinson, he was, on the contrary, commissioned to display to the viceroy *the great pecuniary sacrifices* made by that general, to frustrate the plan of invasion meditated by the Ex-Vice-President against the kingdom of Mexico, and to solicit, in consideration of such important services, a pretty round sum of at least *two hundred thousand dollars*.†

Don Joseph de Yturrigaray received this communication with due contempt and indignation, bidding his interpreter to tell Mr. Burling that General Wilkinson, in counteracting any treasonable plan of Mr. Burr, did no more than comply with his duty; that he (the viceroy) would take good care to defend the kingdom of Mexico against any attack or invasion; and that he did

---

* Martin's History of Louisiana.

† Correspondence of Maria Ines Jauregui de Yturrigaray, Vice-queen. Davis's Life of Burr, vol. ii. p. 401.

not think himself authorized to give one farthing to Gen. Wilkinson, in compensation for his pretended services. He, thereupon, ordered Burling to leave the city of Mexico, and had him safely escorted to the port of Vera Cruz, where he embarked for New Orleans.

On the seventh of December, previous, Wilkinson had despatched Lieutenant Swann, of the army, to Jamaica, with a letter to the officer commanding the naval force on that station, informing him of Burr's plans, and that a report was afloat that the aid of a British naval armament had been either promised or applied for. He therefore warned him, and all other British military and naval officers, that their interference, or any co-operation on their part, would be considered as highly injurious to the United States, and affecting the then present amicable relations between the two nations. The communication concluded with a hope, that the British government would refrain from any interference, and prevent individuals from affording aid to the enterprise; assuring him that the writer would, with all the force under his command, resist any effort of a foreign power to favour Burr's projects.

To this Admiral Drake replied, that, from the style and manner in which the communication was written, he was at a loss how to answer it; but begged him, (Wilkinson,) to be assured, that British ships of war would never be employed in any improper service, and that he should ever be ready most cheerfully to obey the orders of his sovereign. Sir Eyre Coote trusted, and sincerely believed, the representations made to Wilkinson were totally groundless, as his letter contained the only intelligence received on the subject.*

Bollman and Swartwout were conducted to the city of Washington for trial. After having been imprisoned, for some time, on the charge of treason, as joint-conspirators with Burr, they were discharged from confinement, by order of the Supreme Court, as the evidence was not sufficient to retain them longer in custody.

Ogden and Alexander were transported to Baltimore, as accomplices in the same crime. The former of these was taken before a magistrate, in the city, and set at liberty for want of sufficient proof. The latter was shortly after released, in Washington, whither he had been recently conducted, because of the improper averment of the offence.

---

* Martin's History of Louisiana.

CHAPTER X.

Burr's arrival in the village of Wakefield, Alabama—Inquires for Colonel Hinson's—His conduct excites suspicion—He is pursued by Nicholas Perkins and Brightwell, the Sheriff—Is found at Hinson's—His agreeableness—Suspicions of the Sheriff—Mrs. Hinson's inquisitiveness—His departure from Hinson's—Delinquency of Brightwell—Perkins sets out for Fort Stoddard to procure assistance of Lieutenant Edmund P. Gaines—They start in pursuit—Burr is arrested—His imprisonment at the Fort—Kindness to George S. Gaines—Amusements at the Fort—Burr's travelling companion, Major Ashley, arrested, and escapes—Difficulties in procuring a guard to convey Burr to Richmond—Burr leaves the Fort under guard—Sympathy of the ladies—Guard—Perkins fears the influence of Burr—Particulars of the journey—Burr attempts to escape at Chester—Is unsuccessful—Arrives at Richmond, Virginia.

LATE at night, about the last of February, Burr, with a companion, arrived at a small log tavern, in what is now the village of Wakefield, in Washington county, Alabama. Without alighting, he called at the door, and inquired of the inmates if Colonel Hinson resided in the neighbourhood. Receiving for answer that he did, they further informed him that the house was seven miles distant; the road to be travelled, obscure and difficult; and a deep and turbid creek lay in the route. Nothing daunted, he eagerly sought information as to the forks, and directions as to crossing the stream. This having been communicated, he put spurs to his horse, leaving the observers involved in astonishment.

Near midnight, the glimmering of a light, through the distant trees, directed the travellers to the rude but comfortable quarters of Colonel Hinson. Having hailed and received no answer, they dismounted, and entered the kitchen, where the remaining embers in the fire-place were soon kindled into a comfortable blaze. Seating himself before it, Burr left his companion to take charge of the horses, and had but just begun to feel comfortable, when he was interrupted by a stranger, who, he concluded, had ridden till late to reach desirable lodgings. But in this he was mistaken. The real cause of his appearance, at this unseasonable hour, originated in Burr's mysterious departure from the inn. As it afterwards appeared, Colonel Nicholas Perkins observed, by the light of the fire, as Burr sat upon his horse, that, although he was coarsely dressed, yet he possessed a countenance of unusual intelligence; an eye of sparkling brilliancy; and a demeanor wholly unsuited to the garb he wore. The tidy boot, in particular, which his vanity could not surrender, with his other articles of finer clothing, attracted Perkins's attention, and led him to conclude that the gentleman before him was none other than the famous Colonel Burr, described in the proclamation of the governor.

Perkins immediately started after Theodore Brightwell, the sheriff, who occupied an adjacent cabin; and, awakening him from his slumbers, hurriedly communicated the circumstances of the traveller's appearance, conversation and departure, and requested him to join him in the pursuit of the parties. Brightwell consented; and the two, mounting their horses, took the road to Hinson's. The night was cold and windy, and the moanings of the lofty pines, along the solitary road, rendered their journey gloomy and unpropitious. Still they pressed on; for the object of their pursuit was of no small importance, at that particular time, to the minions of the government. As they arrived in sight of the illuminated dwelling, Perkins, recollecting that the travellers had seen him at the tavern, declined entering, but sent Brightwell, whom he requested to return to him, at a certain place in the woods, after he had ascertained whether or not the suspicious individual was Aaron Burr.

As Brightwell called at the door, his voice

was recognised by Mrs. Hinson, who was his relative, and who until now had remained silent in another room, through fear of the strangers, in the absence of her husband. She soon prepared something to eat for her unknown guests. As Burr seated himself at the table, he thanked her, in the most courteous terms, for her kindness, and apologized for the trouble he had imposed upon her. His conversation was sprightly and agreeable, so much so, indeed, that Mrs. Hinson soon discovered that the gentleman and his attire did not correspond. His attention was often directed to Brightwell, who stood before the fire, and at whom he cast the keenest glances, evidently endeavouring to read his thoughts. A momentary separation having taken place, during the night, between Burr and his companion, at the suggestion of Brightwell, the latter was asked by Mrs. Hinson if she had the honour of entertaining, as her guest, the celebrated Col. Burr. Fearing to make the disclosure, the man remained silent, and shortly after left the room.

Early in the morning, Burr privately communicated to Mrs. Hinson his real name, and regretted the absence of her husband, whom he had seen at Natchez, and with whom he had promised himself to remain a week; but that, as he was now discovered, he should prosecute his journey.

After inquiring the route to Pensacola, and Mrs. Carson's ferry on the Tombigbee, he called for writing materials, and indited several letters. His companion, who had been despatched on the back route, for some purpose, returned about nine o'clock, and the two again set out for the "cut off," not very far distant.

For some unaccountable reason, which has never yet been explained, Brightwell neglected to return to Perkins, whom he left highly excited and shivering in the cold. Having remained at his post until his patience was exhausted, and supposing that Brightwell, probably on account of the fascinations of Burr, or the pity which had seized him, in his behalf, had betrayed their plans, Perkins mounted his horse, and rode rapidly to the house of Joseph Bates, at Nannanhubby Bluff, to avoid the creek, which intervened on the main route to Fort Stoddart. Here he was furnished with a canoe, and a negro to navigate it; and, descending the Tombigbee, arrived at the military station early in the morning. The late General Edmund P. Gaines was then the lieutenant in command. Perkins briefly acquainted him with the particulars of the preceding night's adventure, and of his suspicions; which, although of slight foundation, had nevertheless impressed him with solid convictions of truth. Placing himself at the head of a file of mounted soldiers, the lieutenant started in pursuit, accompanied by Perkins. They shortly encountered the object of their search, with his travelling companion, and the sheriff, Brightwell. The parties having met, Lieutenant Gaines accosted one of the strangers, remarking, that he presumed he had the honour of addressing Colonel Burr.

"I am a traveller," answered Burr, "and in a strange land, and do not recognise your right to ask such a question."

"I arrest you, at the instance of the United States," replied Gaines.

"By what authority do you arrest me, a stranger, on the highway, on my own private business?"

The lieutenant then informed Burr that he was an officer of the United States army, and held in his hand the proclamation of the President, as well as that of the Governor of the Mississippi Territory, directing his arrest.

Burr asked him if he was aware of the responsibility of arresting a traveller; to which Gaines answered, that he was perfectly aware of his duties, in the premises, and should endeavour to perform them.

Burr then entered into a brief argument to show that these proclamations should never have been issued, and that in following their dictates, the lieutenant would be subjecting himself to much damage and blame. His manner was firm; his air majestic; and his language impressive; but the resolute young officer told him his mind was made up;—the prisoner must accompany him to his quarters, where he would be treated with all the respect due the Ex-Vice-President of the United States, so long as he made no attempt to escape. He was then conducted towards Fort Stoddart, where the parties arrived in the evening, and an apartment being assigned the prisoner, he took his dinner alone.

Late at night, a groaning was heard, in an adjoining room. Burr arose, opened the door, and ascertained that George S. Gaines was suffering from severe indisposition. He approached the sufferer's bed and kindly offered his services, as he had travelled much, and had some knowledge of medicine. They soon entered into a sprightly conversation in regard to the state of the country, and particularly on the subject of the Choctaw Indians, among whom Gaines lived, as United States factor. The next day, being introduced to the wife of the commandant, who was a daughter of the late Judge Toulman, Burr dined with the family, and enlivened the company with his wit and elegant discourse. In the evening, he played chess with Mrs. Gaines, with whom he was often a frequent competitor in that interesting game. Of nights, he sought the company of the invalid, who became exceedingly attached to his society. During their midnight conversations, how often would the good heart of his auditor grieve over the misfortunes of Burr. But it was a remarkable fact, that, as often and long as they were together, this unfortunate man never once alluded to his arrest, his troubles, or his future plans. From his early youth, it had been his custom to conceal things in relation to himself, and he always endeavoured to throw an air of mystery over his acts.

After Burr had been secured, as a prisoner at Fort Stoddart, Perkins departed for Wakefield, and caused the arrest of his travelling companion, who proved to be Major Ashley. He was placed under a guard, from whom he escaped and made his way to Tennessee, where he afterwards made himself serviceable to his friend, in collecting evidence in his behalf for the trial at Richmond.

Three weeks had passed away since the arrest of the distinguished prisoner, and still the lieutenant had been unable to convey him to the seat of the general government for trial. The difficulties were great, and, for a time, the undertaking appeared impracticable. In those days, there were comparatively no roads, no ferries, and few men could be found, in that sparsely settled country, who would undertake a journey so long and perilous, over savage lands. The inclemency of the weather, at that season of the year, added much to the unpleasantness of the tour, and, with many, formed an insuperable objection, as they must, necessarily, for want of houses of accommodation, be exposed, both night and day, to the vicissitudes of the month of March. At last, Burr left the fort, under guard, and proceeded, in a government boat, up the Alabama river, into the Tensaw lake, accompanied by Lieutenant Gaines, and stopped at the house of John Mills. The ladies of the house, seeing the strait to which Burr was reduced, wept, through sympathy for his misfortunes. One of the number, it is said, a Mrs. Johnson, named her son in honour of this distinguished individual. He is still alive, and is not the only boy bearing the name of "Aaron Burr" in the State of Mississippi. The ladies everywhere espoused his cause, in the south-western New World. It is a prominent and noble trait, in female character, to admire a man of daring and generous impulses, and to pity and defend him in his adversities.

At the boat-yard, in the present county of Baldwin, in the State of Alabama, the crew disembarked, where William and John Pierce, (who introduced the first cotton gins into Alabama,) had a trading establishment. Gaines gave the command of the guard to Perkins, and directed him to convey the prisoner to Washington city. His guard consisted of Thomas Malone, of Alabama, Henry B. Slade of North Carolina, two McCormacks of Kentucky, and two United States' soldiers. They were all men whom Perkins selected, and upon whom he could rely under every circumstance. He took them aside, and obtained the most solemn pledges, that, upon the whole route to Washington, they would hold no interviews with Burr, nor suffer him to escape alive. Perkins knew the fascinations of Burr, and he feared his familiarity with his men, indeed, he feared the same influences upon himself. His character, for making strong impressions upon the human mind, and attaching men to him by association, was well known to the world.

When Burr fled from the authorities in the Mississippi Territory, he had disguised himself in a boatman's dress. His pantaloons were of coarse, copperas-dyed cloth, with a roundabout of inferior drab. His hat, a flapping, wide-brim beaver, had, in times long past, been white, but now gave evidence of having encountered much rough weather. Placed upon his fine horse, he bestrode him most elegantly, and flashed his large, dark eyes, as though he were at the head of his New York regiment. Each man carried provisions for himself, and some for the prisoner. They were all well mounted, with no arms except pistols in holsters, and two muskets borne by the soldiers. On the last of February, they set out upon their long and perilous journey. Within a quarter of a mile from the point of departure, the dreadful massacre at Fort Mimms occurred, six years after. Pursuing the Indian path, which led from the "'Bigby settlement," to Fort Wilkinson, on the Oconee, they reached a point thirty miles distant the first day. At night, the only tent in the company was pitched for the prisoner, who reposed himself upon his blankets. The country abounded in immense pine forests. Here the Ex-Vice-President lay the first night, before the blazing fire, which threw a glare over the dismal woods.

To what an extremity had he now been reduced! In the boundless wilds of Alabama,—under a small and comfortless tent; amid the perils of Indian barbarities, with the cry of the panther, answered by the howl of the hungry wolf ringing in his ears; while the moaning of the winds through the tops of the lofty trees added dreariness to the solitude of the night. With none with whom to hold converse; surrounded by a guard to whom he dared not speak; a prisoner of the United States for whose liberties he had fought, and whose government he had helped to form; exiled from the State of his adoption, whose statutes and institutions bore the impress of his mind; deprived by death of his devoted wife; his only child then on a distant coast of Carolina; his professional pursuits abandoned, and his fortune swept away; the magnificent scheme of the conquest of Mexico uprooted, and the fragments dispersed; slandered and hunted down, from one end of the Union to the other; these were considerations sufficient to weigh down an ordinary individual, and sink him to an untimely grave. But his was no common mind; and the characteristic fortitude and determination which had ever marked his course, still sustained him in the darkest hour. In the morning, he arose cheerfully, and pursued his course. Although guarded with vigilance, his few wants were gratified, as far as they could be, and he was treated with respect and kindness. The trail being narrow and obscure, Burr rode in the middle, having a part of the guard in front, while the rest followed behind, in single file. The route lay about eight miles south of the present city of Montgomery, then an Indian town called Eaconcharte—meaning *Red Ground*.

In the year 1811, General Wade Hampton cut out the "Federal Road" along this trail, which was well known to early settlers as the only highway in South Alabama. The guard passed by the site of the present Mount Meigs, and stopped at the house of "Old Milly," the former wife of a British soldier, who, with her husband, in 1770, left the barracks in Savannah and came to the Creek nation. She had long been a resident of these wild woods, now lying in the county of Montgomery. Her husband, at this time a coloured man, named Evans, was employed by Perkins to pilot the party across the dangerous creeks, Lime, Dubahatchee and Calabee, all of which they had to swim. It was a perilous and fatiguing march; and, for days, the rain descended in chilling torrents on these unsheltered horsemen, collecting in rivulets and swimming them at every point. Hundreds of Indians thronged the trail, and the party could have been shot down; but the fearless Perkins bore on his distinguished prisoner, amid angry elements and human foes. In their journey through Alabama, they always slept in the woods, near swamps of reeds, upon which the belled and hobbled horses fed during the night. After a hastily-prepared breakfast, it was their custom again to remount, and march on, in gloomy silence, which was but occasionally broken by a remark about the weather, the creeks, or the horses. Burr was a splendid rider, sitting firmly in the saddle, and ever on the alert. He was always a hardy traveller, and although wet for hours, with cold and drizzling rains, riding forty miles a day, and at night stretched upon the bare ground, on a thin pallet, yet, in the whole distance to Richmond, he was never heard to say that he was sick, or even fatigued. At the Chattahoochie, was a crossing-place, owned by an Indian named Marshall. The effects of the expedition were carried over in canoes, while the horses swam alongside. In this manner, they passed the Flint and Ocmulgee. At Fort Wilkinson, on the Oconee, they entered the first ferry-boat they had seen on the whole route. A few miles further on, they were sheltered by the first civilized roof—a house of entertainment, kept by one Bevin. While breakfast was preparing, and the guard were seated around a large fire, the host, like all publicans on the highway, inquired from whence they came. As they were from the "'Bigby settlements," he immediately fell on the fruitful theme of the *traitor*, Aaron Burr. He asked if he had been taken? "Was he not a very bad man?" "Wasn't everybody afraid of him?" Perkins and his party were very much annoyed, and embarrassed, and made no reply. Burr was sitting in a corner, by the fire, with his head down; and, after listening to the inquisitiveness of Bevin until he could endure it no longer, he raised himself up, and, planting his fiery eyes upon him, said:

"I am Aaron Burr; what is it you want with me?"

Bevin, struck with his appearance,—the keenness of his look, and the solemnity and dignity of his manner, stood aghast, and trembled like a leaf. He uttered not another word, while the guard remained at his house.

When Perkins reached the confines of South Carolina, he watched Burr more closely than ever; for, in this State lived the son-in-law of Burr, Col. Alston, a gentleman of talents, wealth and influence; and afterwards governor of the State. Upon reaching the frontiers of Georgia, he endeavoured to convey the prisoner in by-roads, to avoid the towns, lest he should be rescued. The plan was attended with difficulty; they were lost often; the march impeded; and the highway was again resumed. Before entering the town of Chester, in South Carolina, the party halted. Two men were placed before Burr; two on either side, and two behind; and in this manner, they passed near a tavern on the street, where many persons were standing; while music and dancing were heard in the house. Burr conceived it a favourable opportunity for escape, and, suddenly dismounting, exclaimed,

"I am Aaron Burr, under military arrest, and claim protection of the civil authorities!"

Perkins leaped from his horse, with several of his men, and ordered him to remount.

"*I will not!*" replied Burr.

Not wishing to shoot him, Perkins threw down his pistols, and, being a man of prodigious strength, and the prisoner a small man, seized him around the waist and placed him in his saddle, as though he was a child. Thomas Malone caught the reins of the bridle, slipped them over the horse's head, and led him rapidly on. The astonished citizens had seen a party enter their village, with a prisoner; had heard him appeal to them for protection; had witnessed the feat of Perkins; and the party vanished, before they had time to recover from their confusion; for, when Burr dismounted, the guards cocked their pistols, and the people ran within the piazza to escape from danger.

Burr was still, to some extent, popular in South Carolina; and any wavering or timidity, on the part of Perkins, would have lost him his prisoner; but the celerity of his movements gave no time for the people to reflect, before he was far in the outskirts of the village. Here, the guard halted. Burr was highly excited; he was in tears! The kind hearted Malone also wept, at seeing the uncontrollable despondency of him who hitherto had proven almost iron-hearted. It was the first time any one had ever seen Aaron Burr unmanned.

The guard became very much alarmed, on the subject of Burr's rescue, Malone and Henry advised the purchase of a carriage. The former took charge of the guard, while Perkins returned and purchased a gig. The next day, Burr was placed in a vehicle, and driven, without further incident, to Fredericksburg, Virginia. Here Perkins received despatches from the President, requiring him to convey the prisoner to Richmond. The guard took the stage, and soon reached that place. The ladies of the city vied with each other in contributing to the comfort of Burr. Some sent him fruit; some clothes;

some wine; some one thing; some another. Perkins and his men went to Washington; were paid for their services, and returned to Alabama, by way of Tennessee.*

* The whole of the incidents related in the foregoing chapter are taken from Pickett's History of Alabama. With but few exceptions, I have followed nearly the exact language of that author.

CHAPTER XI.

Blennerhassett sets out from Natchez to visit his island—Tarries at Lexington, Kentucky—Arrested by the authorities—Mrs. Blennerhassett's letter—Defended by the Hon. Henry Clay—Is unsuccessful in procuring his discharge—Is conducted to Richmond—Postponement of the trials of Burr and his accused confederates—Trial of Burr commenced—Court and bar—Verdict of acquittal by the jury—Burr's arraignment on an indictment for a misdemeanor—Acquittal—Extracts from Blennerhassett's journal kept during the trial—Extracts from the private memoranda—Chief Justice Marshall—Luther Martin—William Wirt—Aaron Burr.

BLENNERHASSETT having been arrested and discharged in the Mississippi territory, imagined no further annoyance from the government. Feeling desirous to ascertain the situation of his property at the island, which he had learned from his wife and others was much injured by the proceedings of the Wood county militia, he left Natchez in June, with the intention of visiting it.

On the route, he stopped at Lexington, Kentucky, where he had many acquaintances and friends, to rest himself, for a time, from the weariness of his journey, and to partake of the hospitalities of its citizens. In the meanwhile, on the twenty-fifth of June, indictments had been preferred, at Richmond, both against Burr and himself; information of which having been received in the village, he was arrested by the authorities, and confined in prison.

If any thing was calculated to wound a heart of the most refined feeling and acutest sensibility, it certainly was this last act of the unrelenting government. In the presence of those from whom he had heretofore received the most courteous attention, and by whom he had been regarded with unusual respect, dragged to the gloomy walls of a prison, and treated as a felon, was humiliating in the most painful degree.

Mrs. Blennerhassett, hearing of his mortifying situation, and feeling the necessity of sustaining him, by her consoling counsel, under the increased weight of his misfortunes, addressed him the following communication:—

NATCHEZ, August 3d, 1807.*

MY DEAREST LOVE.—After having experienced the greatest disappointment in not hearing from you for two mails, I, at length, heard of your arrest, which afflicts me because it *was* an arrest. I think that had you, of your own accord, gone to Richmond and solicited a trial, it would have accorded better with your pride, and you would

* William Wallace. "American Review," 1845.

have escaped the unhappiness of missing my letters which I wrote every week to Marietta. God knows what you may feel or suffer, on our account before this reaches you, to inform you of our health and welfare in every particular; and, knowing this, I trust and feel your mind will rise superior to every inconvenience that your present situation may subject you to. Let no solicitude whatever, for us, damp your spirits. We have many friends here, who do the utmost in their power to counteract any disagreeable sensation occasioned by your absence. I shall live in the hope of hearing from you, by the next mail; and entreat you, by all that is dear to us, not to let any disagreeable feelings, on account of our separation, enervate your mind at this time. Remember, that all here will read, with great interest, any thing concerning you; but still, do not trust too much to yourself: consider your want of practice at the bar, and spare not the fee of a lawyer. Apprize Colonel Burr of my warmest acknowledgments, for his own and Mrs. Alston's kind remembrance; and tell him to assure her she has inspired me with a warmth of attachment which never can diminish. I wish him to urge her to write to me.

God bless you!—prays your

M. Blennerhassett.

Having procured the eminent services of the Hon. Henry Clay, to aid his release from the process of the court, Mr. Blennerhassett relied on his former acquittal; but, notwithstanding the superior forensic abilities of his counsel, the court refused his application, and he found himself constrained to proceed under guard to Richmond, to be tried for the offence of treason.

For various reasons, which it is not necessary here to enumerate, the trials of Burr, Blennerhassett, Dayton, John Smith of Ohio, Comfort Tyler, Israel Smith of New York, and Davis Floyd, were postponed, from time to time, until the third of August. From the fifth until the seventeenth of the month, the court was engaged in obtaining a jury for the trial of Burr, and discussing points of law.

Never before, in the history of the country, was witnessed so grand a display of legal acumen and forensic talent. Upon the bench sat the venerated Marshall—spotless in purity; and, for soundness of judgment, without an equal. Calm, dignified and attentive, he analyzed the arguments of counsel, and noted their relevancy with the nicety of a critic. At the bar, was Wirt, whose fervid and soul-thrilling eloquence, even on this very trial, placed him at once among the first of American orators. With a brilliancy of imagination which astonished his auditors, he swayed the minds of the jury with wonderful effect. There, too, was Martin, who had been previously distinguished, in the trial of Judge Chase, before the United States Senate. Every word that he uttered, like a two-edged sword, pierced the arguments of his opponents at every point. There was Hay; always ready to take advantage of suspicious circumstances, and wield them, with tenfold force, against the prisoner. There was Randolph; slow, calculating and careful; building up the vulnerable points of his case against the attacks of his adversaries. There was Botts; facetious and playful; sometimes descending to the ludicrous, but often rising, with convincing argument, to the grand. There was Wickham; dignified and commanding, taking up his subject with a master hand, and holding it to view, in every conceivable light. And there, too, was the prisoner; proudly preeminent, in point of intelligence, to his brethren of the bar. He had been the Vice-President of the United States. He was accused of the highest and darkest crime in the criminal code. He stood before the supreme tribunal of his country, with the eyes of the nation gazing upon him. In the opinion of many, he was already a condemned criminal. He had the talent and tact, and the resources of the government, to contend against. Every faculty of his mind was exerted in his own defence. The magnitude of the charge; the number of persons involved; the former high standing and extraordinary fortunes of the accused; had excited an interest in the community, such as never before had been known. The witnesses against him were mostly officers of the government, with whom, at one time or another, he had been in some way connected.

For twenty-six days, the court was arduously engaged in the investigation of the offence. The evidence of sixty witnesses had to be examined and noted. Meanwhile, there being no suitable quarters in the city, Burr was confined in the Penitentiary, in the suburbs of Richmond. Every day he was marched into court, on foot, escorted by a body-guard of two hundred men, which would have done honour to an eastern prince. On the first of September, the jury returned a verdict;—"that Aaron Burr is not proved to be guilty, under the indictment, by any evidence submitted to us; we, therefore, find him *not guilty.*" Burr objected to the verdict, as being incorrect in point of form, and asked that the same might be given in the usual way—simply, "Not Guilty." Mr. Hay answered, that, in fact, it was a verdict of acquittal; and that it should be entered in the jury's own words.

"There was no precise form of words by which the jury should be governed."

"They have no right to return a written verdict at all," replied Burr; "they have no right to depart from the usual form." He then called for the recital of the common directions given the jury by the clerk. They were read, and end as follows:—

"If you find him guilty, you are to say so: if not guilty; you are to say so, *and no more.*"

"The jury cannot be indulged," said Burr.—"They have defaced a paper belonging to the court, by writing upon it words which they have no right to write. They ought to be sent back." After a short consultation, it was agreed that the simple verdict of "Not Guilty" might be entered on the records of the court.

On the ninth of September, Burr was again arraigned, upon an indictment for a misdemeanor, which consisted of seven counts; the substance of which were, that Aaron Burr did set on foot a military enterprise, to be carried on against the territory of a foreign prince, viz., the province of Mexico, which was within the territory of the King of Spain, with whom the United States were at peace.

After the prosecution had examined some of their witnesses, and the court had decided that the testimony of others was not relevant, the District-attorney made a motion to discharge the jury. To this motion Burr objected; insisting upon a verdict. This was on the fifteenth of the month. The court, being of opinion that the jury could not, in this stage of the case, be discharged, without the consent of the accused, and that they must give a verdict, they accordingly retired, and very soon returned with a verdict of "*Not Guilty.*"

Blennerhassett's journal, kept during these trials, as given by the biographer of Burr,* shows his great admiration of the talents of his associate, and Burr's unyielding attachment to his project.

Extracts from the Journal of Blennerhassett.

"The vivacity of Burr's wits, and the exercise of his proper talents, now [at Richmond] constantly solicited here, in private and public exhibition, while they display his powers and address, at the levee and the bar, must engross more of his time than he can spare from the demands of other gratifications; while they display

* Mathew L. Davis.

him, to the eager eyes of the multitude, like a favourite gladiator, measuring over the arena of his fame, with firm step and manly grace, the pledges of easy victory.

"August 17th, 1807. This led me to praise a pamphlet, *Agrestis*, which Alston yesterday brought me, being two letters on Wilkinson's proceedings at New Orleans, which, for its arrangement and strength, as well as imagery of language, I observed would not be unworthy of a Curran; at the same time, inquiring who was the author. Alston said he was not known. I then repeated the question to Col. McKee, who said it was a friend of ours; at least Mr. Alston was suspected. I mention this trifling occurrence, for the sake of observing, that Alston was now silent, thereby appropriating to himself the merit of the book, which his *wife*, I have no doubt, might produce. To suppose Alston the author would be preposterous.

"August 23d, 1807. My reverie was soon broken in upon, by the appearance of Mr. Douglas with a stranger. I should rather have said, by two apparitions; for it was now near nightfall, and Douglas no sooner appeared than he turned on his heel, saying, 'Colonel Duane, sir,' and ran down stairs. The surprise of this interruption, the stranger, whom I had never before seen, did not suffer to endure long enough to allow me to invoke the 'angels and ministers of grace' for my protection. I was already within the grasp of this Gabriel of the government. He seized my hand, and bade me dismiss my surprise, however natural it might be, on his appearance before me. I handed him a chair, and said, 'I had lived long enough in this country to be surprised at nothing it could produce or exhibit, but yet desired to learn from what cause I had the favour of his visit.' 'Having heard Mr. Douglas observe,' said he, 'that you would be pleased to see me:'—'Sir, Mr. Douglas has made a mistake; he must have meant somebody else.' 'No matter,' continued he: 'having known and seen your present situation, I could not, as a man, as an Irishman,' (here he digressed, to show me how he both was, and was not, an Irishman,) 'I could not leave this town (Richmond) without warning you of the sacrifice now preparing, to appease the government, by your friends, of which you are destined to be the victim. You cannot desire any other key to my meaning than the course the defence has this week taken. But, if you think the government will not cease to pursue that justice they possess the means of ensuring, and suspect, as you ought, the designs of those you have too long thought your friends, it might yet appear no better, on my part, than a nominal service to give you these cautions. I have, therefore, sought you, not to tender you words, but deeds. The only return, on your part, will be that care of yourself which will find a shield in *my honour*' (here he very awkwardly struck his breast, and grinned a ghastly smile) 'and that confidence I can *command* in the government, whose good faith is not misplaced in the zeal I have testified to serve it.'

"To this harangue, he added violent protestations of his wishes to serve me; saying, that, for that purpose, he would put off his journey back to Philadelphia, which otherwise was irrevocably fixed for Wednesday, and would, now or at any time hereafter, go to Washington for me, where *nothing he should ask would be refused him.* In thanking him for the frankness and zeal with which he cautioned me against my friends, and a negligence of my safety, I assured him I was not afraid to meet the prosecution, as I expected I should, before my arrival here, without counsel or friends; but, from present appearances, I was more curious than interested to learn what were those means the said government possessed of insuring justice. Finding, by his answer, that he was now disposed to allure me into a confession, of having written certain papers then in the hands of the prosecutors, I told him, the warmth of his offers to serve me could not make me forget either his situation, or my own, with relation to the government; that I cared not what writings should be charged upon me; that I should admit none till fairly proved, which, if any such should ever appear, I would justify, if necessary, on the scaffold. He now summed up the objects of his mission, (whatever produced it,) with abuse of Burr, Tyler and Smith, *acknowledging that he had been served gratis, by Burr, in the most handsome manner;* that the others were more concerned against the government than I was; but swearing that he believed, if I did not follow his advice, they would make a scape-goat sacrifice of me for their deliverance.

"August 25, 1807. I asked Alston, 'Would you wish to see my notes of what passed between Duane and me?' 'Yes,' said he, 'very much.' I then read to him the minutes I had taken on Sunday evening, with which he seemed highly pleased, and said they ought to be published. To this, I told him, I could not accede. . . . . I informed him that Duane had intimated that government had got possession of one of his letters to me. 'One of my letters!' cried he. 'I never wrote to you but two upon private business; and, by G—d! any other letter they can have of mine must be a forgery.' 'To be sure,' said I; 'or, at all events, from the favourable course things are now likely to take, such a letter could do no harm! But, what did the rascal,' continued he, 'state to be the purport of the letter?' 'Nothing more,' said I, 'than that you and myself were all equally involved in all Colonel Burr's projects.' He then abused Duane, and repeated his wish that my notes were published.

"September 13th, 1807. I visited Burr this morning. He is gay as usual, and as busy in speculations on re-organizing his projects for action, as if he had never suffered the least interruption. He observed to Major Smith and me, that, in six months, our schemes could be all remounted; that we could now new-model them, in a better mould than formerly, having a better view of the ground, and a more perfect knowledge of our men. We were silent. It should yet be granted, that, if Burr possessed sensibility of the right sort, with one hundredth part of the energies for which, with many, he has obtained such ill-grounded credit, his first and last determination, with the morning and the night, should be the destruction of those enemies who have, so long and so cruelly, wreaked their malicious vengeance upon him.

"September 16th, 1807. I was glad to find Burr had, at least, thought of asking us to dine with him, as I was rather curious to see him shine in a *partie quarrie,* consisting of new characters. We, therefore, walked with him, from court. Luther Martin, who lives with him, accompanying us. . . . . The dinner was neat, and followed by three or four sorts of wine. Splendid poverty! During the chit-chat, after the cloth was removed, a letter was handed to Burr, next to whom I sat. I immediately smelt musk, Burr broke the seal, put the cover to his nose, and then handed it to me, saying, 'This amounts to a disclosure.' I smelt the paper, and said, 'I think so.' The whole physiognomy of the man now assumed an alteration, and vivacity that, to a stranger, who had never seen him before, would have sunk full fifty years of his age. 'This,' said he, 'reminds me of a detection once very neatly practised upon me at New York. One day, a lady stepped into my library, while I was reading, came softly behind my chair, and, giving me a slap on the cheek, said, 'Come, tell me directly what little French girl, pray, have you had here?' The abruptness of the question and surprise left me little room to doubt the discovery had been completely made. So, I thought best to confess the whole fact; upon which the inquisitress burst out into a loud laugh, on the success of her artifice, which she was led to play off upon me, from the mere circumstance of having smelt musk in the room.' I have given this anecdote a place here, only to convey an idea of that temperament and address which enables this character to uphold his ascendency over the sex. After some time, Martin and Provost withdrew, and we passed to the topics of our adventures on the Mississippi, in which Burr said little, but declared he did not know of any reason to blame General Jackson, of Tennessee, for any thing he had done or omitted. But, he declares, he will not lose a day, after the favourable issue at the Capitol, (his acquittal,) of which he has no doubt, to direct his entire attention to setting up his projects, (which have only been suspended,) on a better model, 'in which work,' he says, 'he has even here made some progress.'

"September 20th, 1807. I found Burr, just after a consultation with his counsel, secretly writhing under much irritation at the conduct of Judge Marshall, but affecting an air of contempt for his alleged inconsistencies, as Burr asserted he (the judge) did not, for the last two days, understand either the questions or himself; that he had wavered in his opinions, before yesterday's adjournment, and should, in future, be put right by *strong language.* I am afraid to say *abuse,* though I think I could swear he used that word. I learned from Major Smith, to-day, a confirmation of what Colonel de Pestere had also mentioned to me:—that Burr sets off immediately for England, after his liberation, to collect money for re-organizing his projects.

"September 22d, 1807. I have seen a complete file of all the depositions, made before the grand jury, in Burr's possession. It must be confessed, that few other men, in his circumstances, could have procured these documents, out of the custody of offices filled by his inveterate enemies. Burr asserted, to-day, in court, that he expected documents that would disqualify Eaton as a witness.

"September 26th, 1807. Wilkinson, in his examination, confessed, that he had altered the cipher letter, and sworn that there were no alterations.

"Of Dudley Woodbridge,* it must not be concealed from those who may have access to these *notes,* that although he is reported to have given a fair, candid, and, to us, an advantageous testimony, *he has not yet told the whole truth, having*

---

* Former mercantile partner of Blennerhassett, and contractor for building Burr's boats on the Muskingum. The respectability of Mr. Woodbridge is undoubted by all who know him.—AUTHOR.

suppressed my communication to him, of our designs being unequivocally against Mexico; which, I suppose, he kept back because he embraced and embarked in the plan, on the first mention of it to him, though he afterwards receded from it, upon his own reflection, or counsel of others. Such is the address, with which ingratitude and dishonesty are made to pass in the garb of integrity, like tow-cloth under fine muslin.

"October 8th, 1807. I called on Burr this morning, when he, at last, mentioned to me, during a short tête-à-tête, that he was preparing to go to England; that the time was now auspicious for him; and he wished to know whether I could give him letters. I answered that I supposed, when he mentioned England, he meant London, as his business would probably be with people in office; that I knew none of the present ministry, nor did I believe I had a single acquaintance in London. He replied, that he meant to visit every part of the country, and would be glad to get letters to any one. I said I would think of it, that I might discover whether I had any friends there, whom it would be an object worth his attention to know, and took leave. We can only conjecture his designs. For my part, I am disposed to suspect he has no serious intent of reviving any of his speculations in America, or even of returning from Europe if he can get there."

Extracts from the "Private Memoranda" of Blennerhassett, kept while confined at Richmond.[*]

Chief Justice Marshall.

"From whence Burr did not infer that Chief J., will on the present occasion shrink from his duty, as an able judge or a virtuous patriot, to avert the revenge of an unprincipled government, or avoid other trials menaced and preparing for himself, by its wretched partisans. . . . I am certain, whatever insects may have sought the judge's robes, whilst off his back, none will venture to appear upon the ermine which bedecks his person."

Luther Martin.

"As we were chatting, after dinner, in staggered the whole rear-guard of Burr's forensic army—I mean, the celebrated Luther Martin, who yesterday concluded his fourteen hours' speech. His visit was to Major Smith, but he took me by the hand, saying, there was no need of an introduction. I was too much interested, by the little I had seen, and the great things I

---

* Wm. Wallace. "American Review," 1845.

had heard, of this man's powers and passions, not to improve the present opportunity, to survey him, in every light the length of his visit would permit. I accordingly recommended our brandy as superior, placing a pint-tumbler before him. No ceremonies retarded the libation—no inquiries solicited him upon any subject, till apprehensions of his withdrawing suggested some topic to quiet him on his seat. Were I now to mention only the subjects of law, politics, news, et cetera, on which he descanted, I should not be believed, when I said his visit did not exceed thirty-five minutes. Imagine a man capable, in that space of time, to deliver some account of an entire week's proceedings in the trial, with extracts from memory of several speeches on both sides, including long ones from his own:—to recite half columns *verbatim* of a series of papers, of which he said he is the author;—to caricature Jefferson;—to give a history of his acquaintance with Burr;—expatiate on his *virtues* and sufferings, maintain his credit, embellish his fame, and intersperse the whole with sententious reprobations and praises of several other characters; some estimate, with these preparations, may be formed of this man's powers, which are yet shackled by a preternatural secretion or excretion of saliva which embarrasses his delivery.

In this, his manner is rude, and his language ungrammatical; which is cruelly aggravated upon his hearers, by the verbosity and repetition of his style. With the warmest passions, that hurry him, like a torrent, over those characters or topics that lie most in the way of their course, he has, by practice, acquired the faculty of curbing his feelings, which he never suffers to charge the enemy till broken by the superior numbers of his arguments and authorities, by which he always out-flanks him, when he lets loose the reserve upon the centre, with redoubled impetuosity. Yet fancy has been denied to his mind, or grace to his person or habits. These are gross, and incapable of restraint, even upon the most solemn public occasions. This is, at all times, awkward and disgusting. Hence, his invectives are rather coarse than pointed; his eulogiums more fulsome than pathetic. In short, every trait of his portrait may be given in one word:—he is '*the Thersites of the law.*'"

William Wirt.

"Wirt spoke very much to engage the fancy of his hearers, to-day, without affecting their understanding. For he cannot reason upon the facts before him, and can no more conduct a law argument than I could raise a temple; as Junius says of the king: 'The feather that adorns him supports his flight; strip him of his plumage, and you fix him to earth!'"

Aaron Burr.

"Recurring, with Mr. Smith, to some incidents that happened soon after our first arrival at Natchez, and speaking of Cowles Mead, I was much surprised to learn, what I had never heard before, that Mead had seriously taken up the idea of Col. Burr's being then *deranged*—alleging that he could not be mistaken, as he (Mead) had very long known him. Be this as it may, Burr, yesterday, looked fifty per cent. better than I have ever seen him; and displayed a command of tone and firmness of manner he did not appear to possess before the verdict of Tuesday."

Burr, having been discharged on both indictments, those against Blennerhassett and the others were never prosecuted. Burr and Blennerhassett were required to enter into a recognisance in the sum of three thousand dollars each, for their appearance at Chillicothe, Ohio, to answer to a charge of misdemeanor; "for, that whereas, they prepared an armed force whose destination was the Spanish Territory." Of this, however, no notice was ever taken; thus ended the conspiracy of Burr!

CHAPTER XII.

Origin of the Burr expedition—Miranda's visit in 1797–8—His object —Propositions favourably received—Visits England—Receives encouragement from the British Ministry—Mode of arranging forces for the subjugation of the South American colonies—His plans are defeated by the elder Adams—Burr conceives the plan of the subjugation of Mexico—Auspicious circumstances—Encouragement received from distinguished characters—Wilkinson's aid proffered—His counsel—Daniel Clark—General Jackson—Effect of the adjustment of the Spanish difficulties upon those who at first favoured the expedition—Burr's indomitable perseverance —Treacherous conduct of Wilkinson—Effect of Burr's acquittal upon the public mind—Character of Burr—Belief that Jefferson tacitly assented to the expedition—Circumstances which induce that belief.

MOST, if not all, of the characters involved in the enterprise of Burr, have passed from the theatre of life! Their acts are left to the anxious scrutiny of an impartial posterity. Far be it from us to approach the sanctity of the sepulchre, wilfully to offer an indignity to their remains. But an account of the origin, and an explanation of the circumstances attending that noted event, may not be unacceptable to the readers of the present, while it will doubtless prove a theme of historical interest to those who shall follow us.

The provinces of South America had long felt a desire to resist the authority of Spain. Miranda, a bold and energetic leader, with other of his fellow-patriots, had conceived the design of overthrowing the Spanish dynasty, and establishing, on its ruins, an independent republic. He hoped to procure, as allies, in this herculean undertaking, both the United States and Great Britain. With that view, he visited this country, in 1797–'8, and sought the acquaintance of the most distinguished Americans. Knox and Hamilton, who stood high in influence and official station, favoured his project. He afterwards proceeded to England, and presented himself to the British ministry. They entered into his views. The proposition was that the United States should furnish ten thousand troops, and, in that event, the British government agreed to supply the necessary funds and ships to carry on the expedition. From several communications addressed by Miranda to General Hamilton, it appears that the auxiliary land forces were to be exclusively American, and that of the navy, English. The enterprise would, doubtless, have proceeded, had not the elder Adams, who was at that time President, declined entering into the arrangement.

Burr's attention having been drawn to the subject, he determined to raise an army for the subjugation of Mexico. He had frequent conversations with Jay, who assured him that the boldness of the enterprise would contribute to its success. "From this period," remarks his biographer, "until 1805, Burr's mind seemed constantly engaged in reflecting on the feasibility of the measure, and the proper time for carrying it into effect."

At the period of the commencement of the expedition, various favourable circumstances rendered the undertaking apparently auspicious. The difficulties with Spain, mentioned in a former chapter; the restlessness and disaffection of many of the officers and soldiers of the regular army in the west, who had become tired of a life of inactivity and ease, where there were no amusements to while away their vacant hours, nor fields of battle from whence to pluck the never-fading laurels of conquest; a lack of harmony, not only between the civil and military authorities, but in the ranks of the military themselves; all these considerations might well have flattered Burr that the fates were favourable to the adventurer. "Indeed, I fear treachery has become the order of the day," writes General Jackson to Claiborne. "There is something rotten in the state of Denmark." The facetious McKee, in a communication to Wilkinson, remarks:—"Your letter found me far gone in the blue devils, doubting whether I had better expatriate myself, and try my fortunes amidst the storm now gathering in Europe; however, *nil disperandum, Teucro duce auspice Teucro.* I'll remain here till X'mas."

An extensive correspondence with various distinguished characters of the country, assured Burr of their countenance and co-operation, in the event of a war with Spain. Wilkinson, the commander-in-chief of the forces in the West, writes him, under date of October, 1805:—"I fear Miranda has taken the bread out of your mouth." Wilkinson's regular force consisted only of about six hundred men, around which the followers of Burr were to form. These, in fact, were the only disciplined corps relied on. It is said the commander had pledged himself to strike the blow, whenever it should be deemed expedient. All that was wanting, with him, was a pretext for the commencement of hostilities against Spain. He detailed to Burr all the information he possessed, respecting Mexico, and pointed out the facilities which would probably be offered by the inhabitants in effecting a revolution: "On his suggestion, Daniel Clark twice visited the country. He held conferences, and effected arrangements, with many of the principal military officers, who engaged to favour the revolution. The Catholic Bishop, resident at New Orleans, was also consulted; and prepared to promote the enterprise. He designated the priests of the order of Jesuits as suitable agents, and they were, accordingly, employed. The bishop was an intelligent and social man. He had been in Mexico, and spoke with great freedom of the disaffection of the clergy in South America. The religious establishments of the country were not to be molested. Madam Xavier Tarjcon, superior of the Ursuline nuns at New Orleans, was in the secret. Some of the sisterhood were also employed in Mexico. So far as any decision had been formed, the landing was to have been effected at Tampico."*

Daniel Clark engaged to advance, for the purposes of the expedition, fifty thousand dollars; but, being disappointed, was unable to furnish it. Murray, the British Plenipotentiary resident in the United States, was consulted on the subject. He communicated to his government the project of Burr. Col. Williamson, the brother of Lord Balgray, was despatched to England, on the

---

* Davis's Memoirs of Burr, vol. ii. p. 382.

business. From the manner of his reception, and the encouragement he received, it was expected that a British naval squadron would have been furnished for the enterprise. General Jackson had also been consulted, and funds for defraying the expenses of his division were placed in his hands by Burr. The disaffection of the inhabitants of the South and West was thought favourable to a separation of the trans-Alleghany territory, and this, it is said, was among the earlier schemes of Burr, although but seldom revealed, except to those whom he supposed would favour it.

Such were the preparations:—a plan well-matured, and auguring success, in the event of a war with Spain:—for upon this event alone, let it be remembered, had his principal force consented to join the expedition. As soon, however, as intelligence had been received, that such satisfaction had been rendered, on the part of the Spanish government, as to obviate the necessity of a resort to arms, many of the warmest advocates of the plan abandoned their former designs, and turned their attention to scenes less dazzling but more productive of substantial enjoyment. "I had written a great deal," says McKee, "about recruiting in Tennessee—about cutting and slashing and packing dollars, and enjoying *otium cum dignitate*, but *'all our differences being settled with Spain'* knocks all my Utopia to the devil!"

Burr had dreamed too long of the wealth and splendour of the halls of the Montezumas, to resign their captivating pleasures for the tamer scenes of a government in which he was becoming daily more unpopular; and which, he now conceived, viewed his actions with ungrateful suspicions. For years, had he cherished the hope of investing himself with the regal power of that ancient kingdom, and transmitting its crown to his latest posterity. For the realization of this, had he sacrificed the comforts of home; traversed the States to the extremes of Florida; often travelling through pathless wildernesses, sometimes without shelter, and occasionally without food, alluring to his standard men of every grade, prompted by every motive of action.

Confident of the aid of Wilkinson, and the forces under his command, he continued his exertions, after every prospect of a war with Spain had ceased. Whatever motive may have influenced the subsequent conduct of that officer, there is but little doubt that he had given Burr the most indubitable assurance of his firm adhesion to the undertaking. In the vagueness of conjecture, charity would, indeed, suggest such reasons for the change, as usually actuates the soldier and the patriot; but, unfortunately opposed to this conclusion, is his demand of the Spanish viceroy, of the sum of two hundred thousand dollars, "for great pecuniary sacrifices, in defeating Burr's plans, and, Leonidas-like, throwing himself in the pass of Thermopylæ."

Notwithstanding the suspicions with which his movements were observed by the government, the acts of the Ohio legislature, and his arrest in Kentucky, Burr still persisted in his measures; giving confidence to his followers by his unflinching determination. Even the proclamation of the President, and of the several Governors within the respective States and Territories along his route, could not deter him. But, when he was informed that the measures adopted by the government for his arrest were through the advice and at the instance of Wilkinson; that *he* had not only proved treacherous by exposing the scheme and magnifying its object, but was the chosen instrument for his arrest; that courage, which had before characterized his actions, completely abandoned him; then, and not till then, did he sink under the accumulated difficulties which beset his path.

He was arrested, tried and acquitted, "but his country refused to believe him innocent. Though stout old Truxton had testified in his favour;

though Jackson had seen nothing wrong in Burr's project, but agreed to favour it; the popular voice continued to regard him as a traitor, whom accident alone had prevented from dismembering the Union. That a man of sense and ability should entertain such a notion; relying for aid on associates whom he knew would countenance no treason, is a preposterous and insane supposition. As he said, on his death-bed, he might as well have attempted to seize the moon and parcel it out among his followers.

"The real secret of the popular belief is to be found in the character of Burr. In him, the elements which make great and good men were strangely mixed up with those which we may suppose the spirits of evil to pride themselves. He was brave, affable, munificent, of indomitable energy, of signal perseverance. In his own person, he combined two opposite natures. He was studious, but insinuating; dignified, yet seductive. Success did not intoxicate, nor reverse dismay him. Turning to the other aspect of his character, these great qualities sunk to insignificance, beside his evil ones. He was profligate in morals, public and private; selfish and artful; a master in dissimulation, treacherous, cold-hearted. Subtle, intriguing, full of promise; he shot upwards in popularity, with astonishing velocity; but a skeptic in honesty, a scorner of all things noble and good, he failed to secure the public confidence, and fell headlong from his dizzy eminence. Here lies the secret of his ruin. There was nothing in his character to which the great heart of the people could attach itself in love; but they shrank from him, in mistrust, as from a cold and glittering serpent. The public rarely errs in an estimate like this."

It has been alleged of Mr. Jefferson, that he was privy to Burr's arrangements; and that they were tacitly assented to by him. In viewing the various circumstances—particularly the conduct of the President himself—it would appear that such an allegation was not altogether groundless. Burr had been a formidable rival, in his master-struggle, for the Presidency. It had required thirty ballotings to decide the question between them, and Jefferson's final success was owing to a compromise of the members of the Senate, by which the votes of Vermont, Delaware and Maryland were withdrawn from the opposition, through no particular preferences for the latter, but to conciliate parties and silence the exciting topic. If Burr's political aspirations could receive another direction, it is presumed that his ambitious opponent would offer no objections, provided success would place him beyond the circle of his own operations. Indeed, it had been suggested that he should be offered a foreign mission, that his influence at home might not cripple the affairs of the administration.

The subject of the conquest of Mexico was daily conversed upon by the officers of the various Departments, as is clearly established by the evidence on the trial. The Spanish war was a theme of universal interest, and had that event happened, what cared the President whether the American forces paused on the banks of the Sabine, or carried their arms into the heart of Mexico. Already had arrangements been effected between the government and the Spanish officers of Louisiana and Florida, by which those officers were to favour the Americans, in case of a war, and rally under the standard of the forces of the Union.* And, such would, doubtless, have been

* "John Smith, a member of the United States Senate from Ohio, who was arrested as an accomplice of Burr, in a conversation with his friends, stated that, before the movements of Burr had attracted general notice, Mr. Jefferson requested a confidential interview with him, (Smith,) at which he inquired if he was not personally acquainted with the Spanish officers of Louisiana and Florida. On being answered in the affirmative, he went on to state, that a war with Spain seemed to be inevitable; and that it was very desirable to know the feelings of those men towards the United States, and whether reliance could be placed on their friendship, if a war should take place between the two countries. At the same time, he requested him to visit the country, with reference to that object. Mr. Smith stated that he did visit the country, as requested; and that,

the case, had a declaration of war been proclaimed; but an intimation from the French ambassador, that the measure would call Napoleon to the aid of Spain, induced the government to abandon its designs, and arrest the operations of Burr.

And again; it was a notorious fact that the most of those who favoured the project before the President's proclamation, were Republicans —the friends of Jefferson, who had but little sympathy with Burr. Party spirit ran high, and measures inimical to the administration would have been instantly checked by its friends. Until the difficulties with Spain had been adjusted, in the opinion of Jefferson's more intelligent adherents, there was nothing frightful in the preparations of Burr. Indeed, it has

on his return, he reported to Mr. Jefferson, that the governor, the inferior officers, and the inhabitants generally, were not only friendly but were desirous of attaching themselves to the United States. This was in the summer preceding the 'war message' against Spain, which was sent to the two Houses of Congress, in December, 1805. Although the message was confidential, it soon became known to the diplomatic corps at Washington; and the French Ambassador was ordered, by his master, (Napoleon,) to inform the American Government that France would take a part with Spain, in any contest she might have with the United States. It is a matter of history, that, after that notice, the project against Spain, communicated in the confidential message and referred to in the conversation with Mr. Smith, was abandoned; and about the same time, measures were taken to stop the movements of Burr.—*Burnet's Notes*, p. 294.

been charged upon the President, that he approved of the project of Miranda; if so, why not also that of Burr? as they both stood upon the same platform, and were equally criminal under the law of nations.

CHAPTER XIII.

Blennerhassett returns to Natchez after the trial—His pecuniary embarrassments—Sacrifice and abuse of his property—His complacency—Demands indemnity for his losses from Gov. Alston—Purchases a farm in Mississippi, and commences the culture of cotton—Mrs. Blennerhassett's assistance—Flattering prospects—Effects of the embargo—Receives the intelligence of the burning of his mansion.

After the close of this memorable trial, which had occupied the public attention for several months, Blennerhassett returned to Natchez. The continued anxiety, attendant on a tedious investigation of the charge of treason in which character and life were involved; the accumulation of debts; the neglect of domestic interests, and the rapid decline of his resources, were discouragements, indeed, under which stouter hearts might well have sunk without the charge of effeminacy.

The creditors, who had advanced funds upon his obligations, finding his pecuniary affairs becoming daily more embarrassed, were insolent and exacting. Liquidation was demanded; and, when they saw that he neither had the funds to meet them, nor the ability to procure further credit, they pursued him with the precepts of the law, with a rapacity, equalled only by their uncharitable invectives. A portion of his library and philosophical apparatus, which had been his amusement in prosperity, and the solace of his darker hours; the remaining furniture possessing value to him, wholly unappreciated by others; were attached and sold at a criminal sacrifice.

His beautiful mansion, together with its surrounding shrubbery, had been regarded and used as public property. Its fair gardens had been destroyed, not less by the hands of the ruthless freebooter than the negligence of his tenants and the floods of the Ohio. Not satisfied with that which might be removed without injury to the freehold, the window-casings were torn out, to procure the leaden weights by which the sashes were raised. Even the beautiful stone roller, used for levelling his grounds, was crushed to pieces, to obtain the iron axles on which it ran. The island itself was extended, by a writ of *elegit*,* at the suit of Robert Miller of Kentucky, who commenced the culture of hemp, and the manufacturing of cordage.

Such is but the every-day lesson of human

* A process by the Virginia statute, which "extends" the lands of the debtor until the claim is made out of rents and profits.

experience!—Such is the sympathy of unfeeling man with the misfortune and distress of his fellow man! To-day, he kneels at the shrine of friendship, as the beastial Caliban at the feet of Stephano, and calls the object of its worship, "god;" to-morrow shrinks cowardly from it, and returns his gratitude, in foul misdeeds and wanton injuries.

In viewing the complacency with which Blennerhassett had heretofore regarded Burr's actions towards himself, we are at a loss whether to attribute his silence to the mildness of his temper, or a lack of courage to vindicate his honour from the aspersions of his enemies. But, for his unfortunate alliance with Burr, he might still have reposed in the shady groves of the isle. But for Burr, he might have continued to enjoy those peaceful pursuits for which he had abandoned Castle Conway, to secure a home in the secluded forests of America; but for him, he might yet have enjoyed a competency beyond his wants, and luxuriated in the fields of literature, without the fear of pecuniary distress.

It was not, however, until driven to it by necessity, that Blennerhassett attempted to show how much he had really been injured by the man whom he had regarded and cherished as his friend; but who had now deserted him in the hour of misfortune. Almost bankrupt in purse, with a large family dependent upon him for support, to whom could he look for indemnity, for the losses sustained in the enterprise of Burr? He had contributed largely, if not entirely, to the procuring of boats, implements and provisions for the expedition, and, as yet, had received nothing in return. Both Burr and Alston had turned a deaf ear to his petitions for relief; indeed, Burr, had it been his desire, could afford but poor satisfaction from the meagre remains of a once large fortune. Blennerhassett, accordingly, addressed a letter to Gov. Alston, demanding of him the sum of thirty-five thousand dollars, stating that, unless he advanced it, the writer would publish a pamphlet, disclosing the governor's connection with Burr. He concludes by adding, "My work is ready for the press. If you do not prevent its publication, you may rest assured I shall not, to save the trouble of smelting, abandon the ore, I have, with such expense of time and labour, extricated from the mines both dark and deep, not indeed of Mexico, but of Burr, Jefferson, and Alston. Having mentioned Burr, I wish you to observe, that I have long since ceased to consider reference to his honour, resources, or good faith, in any other light than as a scandal to any man offering it, who is not sunk so low as himself."* The pamphlet alluded to did not make its appearance; and it was afterwards said, that the sum of ten thousand dollars was forwarded by Alston.

Cotton, at that time, commanded an exorbitant price. Investments in lands adapted to its culture, and slaves to work it, afforded rich returns for the amount of capital employed. Many were turning their attention to it. Blennerhassett conceived it a favourable mode of retrieving his shattered fortune. He therefore concluded a purchase of a thousand acres of land, in Claiborne county, at St. Catherine's, near Gibsonport, Mississippi, and placed upon it a small number of slaves. Here, again, after the varied incidents of two long years, in which he had been buffeted about, by the whirlwind of uncourted excitement, he found a HOME.

Individuals who, from early life, have been accustomed to battle with the vicissitudes of fortune appear to struggle the greater when encountered by opposing difficulties. Those, on the contrary, who have been cradled in the lap of ease, are but poorly prepared to meet adversity, unless endowed by nature with unusual perseverance. This latter quality, it was not

* Burr's private Journal, vol. i. p. 157.

Blennerhassett's fortune to possess. Accustomed not only to the comforts but the elegancies of life, he was a stranger to want. His sleep had never been disturbed by visions of distress; nor his energies excited through cupidity or avarice. It may well be imagined therefore, that he was but slightly qualified to sustain himself, under his present embarrassments. For him, life had but few attractions, save those that were found in the pursuits of science; and to deprive him of these, was to deprive him of the happiness of existence.

With a full appreciation of her husband's feelings, Mrs. Blennerhassett undertook to aid him in the management of his farm. At the early dawn, she mounted her horse, to convey to the overseer the instructions committed to her charge. In this, however, she never neglected the affairs of her household, or those affectionate attentions to her family, which render the felicities of home bright to the recollection of husband and child, when the memory of all else has perished.

The success of his new undertaking animated Blennerhassett in the hope of reclaiming his losses in a very short time. Such, indeed, would have been the result, had not the war of 1812, and the embargo which followed, put a decided check to our commercial transactions. Produce, of every description, immediately fell in price, until the commodity would scarce pay the expenses of marketing. A bare subsistence, therefore, was all he could promise himself, until a termination of hostilities between the contending nations.

But misfortunes seldom come singly. It was but a short time previous, that he had heard of the fate of his island residence, rented, by him, to one of his Belpré friends, but who was, afterwards, dispossessed by the Kentucky creditor. As the beauty of the grounds had been entirely destroyed, and the mansion itself much injured, through carelessness and neglect, it had lost its primitive attractions, and was now regarded as a mere convenience in farming. In the year eighteen hundred and eleven, the tenant raised an unusual quantity of hemp, which was stored in one of the wings of the building. On a very cold night, several of the slaves, who had been permitted to visit their Virginia friends, overturned the boat in which they were returning, and one of their number was drowned. Suffering under intense cold, they proceeded to the cellar where the spirituous liquors were kept, to obtain the stimulus for counteracting the ill effects of their accident. Passing through the entrance of the hemp-room, to which the stairway led, by accident they communicated the flame of the candle to the hemp, and, in a few moments, the destroying element was beyond their control. Stupid with astonishment, at the awfulness of the spectacle, in the darkness of the night, they neglected to apprize the inmates, who would all doubtless have perished, had not some one of them fortunately awakened in time to give the alarm. Escaping, with nothing but their night-clothes, and a few articles of furniture, they beheld, with awe, this beautiful mansion, which, but a few years previous, had been the abode of peace and happiness—adorned with all that could embellish or beautify its appearance, rapidly reduced to a mass of ruins.

CHAPTER XIV.

Blennerhassett's prospects declining—Is offered a judgeship by the Governor of Canada—Sells his estates—Removes to Montreal—Mrs. Blennerhassett's poetry, "The Deserted Isle"—Blennerhassett again disappointed—Determines to prosecute a claim subsisting in Ireland—Sails for Ireland—Reflections—Applies to Lord Anglesey for office—Letter of Mr. Gossett—Is again disappointed—Removes to the island of Guernsey—Death.

TEN years had passed rapidly away, since the occurrences of the "Burr expedition." The prospect of regaining his fortune became daily less flattering to Blennerhassett. His numerous debts had not ceased to be pressed, at the imminent peril of a total sacrifice of his remaining property. While thus surrounded with insuperable difficulties, a ray of hope, for a moment, dissipated the clouds which obscured the future, and thrilled with joy the desponding bosoms of his household. The acting Governor of Canada, an old and intimate acquaintance, hearing of his critical situation, addressed him a communication tendering his assistance. Blennerhassett's legal attainments qualified him for the duties of the Bench;

the Governor knew it, and offered him a seat in one of the provincial courts. With the view of accepting so desirable a post, he disposed of his fee in the island, as well as that of the Mississippi estate, and removed to Montreal, in 1819.

While here, with prospects of poverty and blighted hopes thickening around them, Mrs. Blennerhassett wrote the following lines, descriptive of the island—her once happy home. They are from the overflowing of a heart which had passed through much sorrow, and are an eloquent lament over the misfortunes and ruin of the family and fortune of Blennerhassett.

"THE DESERTED ISLE."

Like mournful echo, from the silent tomb,
That pines away upon the midnight air,
Whilst the pale moon breaks out, with fitful gloom;
Fond memory turns with sad, but welcome care,
To scenes of desolation and despair,
Once bright with all that beauty could bestow,
That peace could shed, or youthful fancy know.

To the fair isle, reverts the pleasing dream;—
Again thou risest, in thy green attire,
Fresh, as at first, thy blooming graces seem;—
Thy groves, thy fields, their wonted sweets respire;
Again thou'rt all my heart could e'er desire.
Oh! why, dear isle, art thou not still my own?
Thy charms could then for all my griefs atone.

The stranger that descends Ohio's stream,
Charm'd with the beauteous prospects that arise,
Marks the soft isles that, 'neath the glittering beam,
Dance with the wave and mingle with the skies,
Sees, also, one that now in ruin lies,
Which erst, like fairy queen, tower'd o'er the rest,
In every native charm, by culture, dress'd.

There rose the seat, where once, in pride of life,
My eye could mark the queenly river's flow,
In summer's calmness, or in winter's strife,—
Swollen with rains, or battling with the snow.
Never, again, my heart such joy shall know.
Havoc, and ruin, rampant war, have pass'd
Over that isle, with their destroying blast.

The black'ning fire has swept throughout her halls,
The winds fly whistling o'er them, and the wave
No more, in spring-floods, o'er the sand-beach crawls,
But furious drowns in one o'erwhelming grave,
Thy hallow'd haunts it water'd as a slave.
Drive on, destructive flood! and ne'er again,
On that devoted isle let man remain.

Too many blissful moments there I've known;
Too many hopes have there met their decay;
Too many feelings now for ever gone,
To wish that thou couldst e'er again display
The joyful colouring of thy prime array:
Buried with thee, let them remain a blot,
With thee, their sweets, their bitterness forgot.

And, oh! that I could wholly wipe away
The memory of the ills that work'd thy fall;
The memory of that all-eventful day,
When I return'd, and found my own fair hall
Held by the infuriate populace in thrall,—
My own fireside blockaded by a band
That once found food and shelter of my hand.

My children (oh! a mother's pangs forbear;
Nor strike again that arrow to my soul;)
Clasping the ruffians in suppliant prayer,
To free their mother from unjust control,
While with false crimes and imprecations foul,
The wretched, vilest refuse of the earth,
Mock jurisdiction held around my hearth.

Sweet isle! methinks I see thy bosom torn;
Again behold the ruthless rabble throng,
That wrought destruction taste must ever mourn.
Alas! I see thee now—shall see thee long;
But ne'er shall bitter feelings urge the wrong,
That, to a mob, would give the censure, due
To those that arm'd the plunder-greedy crew.

Thy shores are warm'd by bounteous suns in vain,
Columbia!—if spite and envy spring,
To blot the beauty of mild nature's reign:
The European stranger, who would fling,
O'er tangled woods, refinement's polishing,
May find, expended, every plan of taste,
His work by ruffians render'd doubly waste.

"Misfortune having marked him for her own," Blennerhassett's anticipated promotion was never realized. The capriciousness of the British ministry had removed from office the sympathizing friend, and he found himself cast hopelessly upon the world, at an advanced age, without health, without energy, and almost destitute of the means of a comfortable subsistence.

As a last resort, he determined to prosecute a reversionary claim, still existing in Ireland, regarded by him with indifference in his more affluent days, but which, now, in his destitute situation, recommended itself strongly to his attention. Through the influence of friends, he hoped, also, to obtain an office under the English government, by which he might the more readily gain the means for conducting the suit.

Under these considerations, he left the Province of Canada, and sailed for Ireland, in 1822. As the receding shores of the American continent were dimly shadowed in the distance, he cast a glance towards the fading scene. A recollection of the past was no pleasing retrospect. A quarter of a century had passed since he had hailed those shores, with buoyant hopes and joyful anticipations of future happiness. To him, it was then a land wherein was to be realized all that was lovely, all that was desirable of earth; a land of freemen, with whom was the abode of peace. Then, he was in the noontide of manhood; blessed with health and a competency beyond his wants. The smile of friendship; the marked and decorous respect with which he was met; the welcome greeting; all gave evidence of lasting enjoyment. But, how mysterious are the dispensations of Providence towards the children of men! He had lived long enough to see every one of those bright hopes perish; his fortune had been lost; his health most seriously impaired; and, to fill the measure of unhappiness, he was branded, by public opinion, with a design of overthrowing the liberties of that government which had allured him across the Atlantic. These were reflections gloomy in the extreme, and still the future was not less cheerless. As the green fields of his native isle broke upon his view, how like the Prodigal Son, who had spent his substance in a foreign shore, did he return to his fatherland. But, for him, alas! there was no "plenty and to spare;" no fatted calf was killed; no fond embrace of anxious friends. In the long space of twenty-five years, how many changes had served to break the ties which bound him to his childhood's home! As again he trod the fields of his former sports, memory turned, with melancholy tenderness, to those boon companions of his earlier years. Where, alas! were they? Nought now remained to identify him with the past; and he stood a stranger on his native land!

Lord Anglesey, one of the heroes of the battle of Waterloo, was then presiding over the office of Ordnance at London. He was the old schoolmate and friend of Blennerhassett. To him, therefore, the latter addressed himself, with the hope of obtaining a situation; and also with a view of procuring a patent, for an "invention" which he deemed of some importance. The result of his applications will be shown from the following correspondence :—*

OFFICE OF ORDNANCE, 9th of June, 1827.

SIR :—I am directed, by the Marquis of Anglesey, to acknowledge the receipt of your letter of the 31st ultimo; and to acquaint you that his lordship will be happy to receive the suggestions which you may have to offer, and will submit them to the consideration of the committee, whose province it is to examine and report upon the various projects brought before this department. With respect to your request, an appointment, Lord Anglesey regrets extremely that the long list of pressing claims, received from his predecessor, and the very limited means of attending to them, will not allow his lordship to hold out any expectation that it will be in his power to offer to your acceptance any appointment.

I have the honour to be, sir,
your most obedient servant,
WM. GOSSETT.

H. Blennerhassett, Esq.

* Wm. Wallace.

What the "invention" was, his papers do not disclose; it is sufficient to state, however, that it met with but little favour.

Having resided a sufficient length of time with a maiden sister in England, to find his plans for the future prostrated, he removed to the island of Guernsey. Here, in the year 1831, wearied with the turmoil of life, he sank to his eternal rest, in the sixty-third year of his age, with his head softly pillowed on that bosom which, for thirty-four years, had throbbed in perfect unison with his own.

CHAPTER XV.

Remarks on the life of Blennerhassett—Mrs. Blennerhassett's destitute situation—Resolves to visit the United States to procure indemnity for spoliations—The reasonableness of such a demand—Visits New York—Presents her petition to Congress—Petition—Robert Emmett's aid—Letter to Mr. Clay—Mr. Clay presents the petition—Report of the Hon. William Woodbridge—Death of Mrs. Blennerhassett—Is buried by Irish females.

THUS has it been attempted to portray the life and character of Blennerhassett. From youth to age, and finally to the grave, we have followed his footsteps, with an interest excited more through our sympathy than our admiration of the man. In his life, there is really nothing remarkable. His scientific acquirements never gave to mankind one single truth, nor devised a plan by which to ameliorate the condition of his race. His is not that fame which bedecks with laurels the brow of the hero; or springs from those actions that the world regards as great and glorious. Of these, indeed, he was never emulous. His native country afforded him the finest fields for military notoriety, and, as for political preferment, the times in which he lived were propitious to the aspirant. The names of many of his compeers will descend to posterity in living colours, as long as down-trodden Ireland shall retain a place on the page of history. That celebrity which attended his name was not of his seeking. His was the peculiar temperament, fitted better for the enjoyments of private life, than the battle-field or the political arena. For this, he resigned magnificence and ease, for obscurity in a western wilderness; and it was here he enjoyed, for a time, that uninterrupted repose which had so long attracted his fancy. There, too, he would have doubtless remained but for the circumstances heretofore narrated.

At the death of her husband, Mrs. Blennerhassett was left with a family of dependent children, for whom her greatest exertions could hardly procure subsistence. Long and arduously she toiled, both mentally and physically, to avoid impending poverty. It was not only necessary that they should be fed and clothed, but it was also important that they should receive such an education, as would, at least, fit them for the business-transactions of life. She had now arrived at an age when elasticity, both of body and mind, were nearly destroyed; and this, of itself, was sufficient to prevent any expectation of future success. Under such gloomy prospects, she resolved to visit the United States, and petition the government for relief.

In this, she is not to be regarded as a mendicant asking for *alms*, but rather as an individual asserting her *rights*;—rights most wantonly violated by the officers of a government pledged to the protection of its citizens. These *quasi* agents of the President had not only detained the boats and stores prepared for the enterprise of Burr, but had actually destroyed the former, and consumed the latter. They had invaded the sanctity of her household, had appropriated to themselves and wasted her provisions, broken her furniture, laid waste the gardens, torn down the fences, and had done serious injury to the mansion. They had put Blennerhassett to an enormous expense, in defending himself at Richmond; they, in fact, had reduced him from affluence to comparative poverty. Was this extraordinary sacrifice to be justified, and its victims to remain unsatisfied from the mere fact that Blennerhassett was *accused* of hostility towards the government? Could such an invasion of private rights have been legalized, if, indeed, he had been proved *guilty* of the acts with which he was charged? The American citizen has cause to rejoice that he lives in a land where his rights are protected by law, and when they are invaded, whether by government or individuals, satisfaction must be equally rendered.

In the year 1842, Mrs. Blennerhassett, with an invalid son, visited New York, and, through the hands of her friends, preferred a petition to Congress. With a meekness of disposition which is remarkable, when we recollect her grievances, she says:—

"Your memorialist does not desire to exaggerate the conduct of the said armed men, or the injuries done by them; but she can truly say, that, before their visit, the residence of her family had been noted for its elegance and high state of improvement; and that they left it in a comparative state of ruin and waste. And, as instances of the mischievous and destructive spirit which appeared to govern them, she would mention, that, while they occupied as a guard-room one of the best apartments in the house, (the building of which cost nearly forty thousand dollars,) a musket or rifle ball was deliberately fired into the ceiling, by which it was much defaced and injured; and that they wantonly destroyed many pieces of valuable furniture. She would also state that, being apparently under no restraint, they indulged in continual drunkenness and riot—offering many indignities to your memorialist and treating her domestics with violence.

"These outrages were committed upon an inoffending and defenceless family, in the absence of their natural protector, your memorialist's husband being then away from home; and that, in answer to such remonstrances as she ventured to make against the consumption, waste, and destruction of his property, she was told, by those who assumed to have the command, that they held the property for the United States, by order of the President, and were privileged to use it, and should use it as they pleased. It is with pain that your memorialist reverts to events, which, in their consequences, have reduced a once happy family, from affluence and comfort, to comparative want and wretchedness; which blighted the prospects of her children, and made herself, in the decline of life, a wanderer on the face of the earth."

Robert Emmett, the son of the celebrated Irish patriot, interested himself in her behalf. He had been the intimate friend of Blennerhassett, and sympathized deeply with his afflicted family. In forwarding her memorial to the Hon. Henry Clay of the United States Senate, he remarks:—"Mrs. Blennerhassett is now in this (New York) city, residing in very humble circumstances, bestowing her cares on a son, who, by long poverty and sickness, is reduced to utter imbecility, both of body and mind; unable to assist her, or provide for his own wants. In her present destitute situation, the smallest amount of relief would be thankfully received by her. Her condition is one of *absolute want*, and she has but a short time left to enjoy any better fortune in this world."

Her statement, with regard to the destruction of her property, and the acts of the officers of the government, were fully corroborated by William Robinson, jun., and Morgan Neville, both of whom were present at the island when the occurrences took place. An estimate of the property destroyed was made out by Dudley Woodbridge, the former partner of Blennerhassett in mercantile transactions, which also accompanied her petition.

It would be presumed that, under such a state of circumstances, the American Congress would not long hesitate in granting her full indemnity for past injuries. Mr. Clay presented the petition, and eloquently advocated its justice. He had known Blennerhassett in the noon-tide of his prosperity, when not a cloud darkened the horizon of his effulgent future; he had visited his rural palace, and regaled himself with the luxuries it afforded. He had partaken of its hospitalities, and been entertained by the sprightly conversation of its inmates. He had witnessed Blennerhassett's arrest, in Kentucky, and manfully exerted himself in his defence. He had afterwards witnessed his declining fortunes; and, when destruction had laid waste his possessions, had wandered over the ruins with feelings of unsuppressed sympathy.

The memorial having been referred to the appropriate committee, of which the Hon. William Woodbridge was chairman, he returned a report, alike honourable to his intelligence and clear sense of justice. He advocated the claim as legal and proper, and one which ought to be allowed, notwithstanding it had been thirty-six years since the events transpired. "Not to do so would be unworthy a wise or just nation."

The claim would doubtless have met with the favour of Congress, had not an event transpired, in the meanwhile, which rendered further action unnecessary. Death had visited the suffering applicant, and relieved her of earthly wants. In an humble abode, in the city of New York, her spirit had silently departed! No soothing hand of a relative fanned her fevered temples, nor wiped from her brow the chilly dews of expiring nature. Within that lonely chamber, it was reserved to strangers to witness the last sad scenes. She, who had been born in affluence;—to whom the world appeared, in early life, as Paradise before the fall; who had been honoured by the attentions of the great, and the praises of the humble; whose heart was ever open to the cries of distress, and whose hands were ever ready to relieve the wants of the needy, had, in her turn, to ask the charities of the world! Although the kindly ministrations of a society of Irish females served, in some measure, to assuage the agonies of her parting hours, still it was hard to die thus destitute and deserted; for

> "On some fond breast the parting soul relies,
> Some pious drops the closing eye requires."

And now, as the sable hearse moved slowly along, followed only by those devoted "sisters of charity," it excited no interest in the passing crowd. No mock pageant indicated the life or station of the deceased. In one of the cemeteries of that city, remains all that is earthly of that once accomplished lady, separated from the tomb of her husband by the wide Atlantic. While on their graves we "drop the tribute of a tear," may we never forget the lesson that their lives have taught us.

APPENDIX.

I.

MRS. THEADOSIA BURR ALSTON.

ONE individual alone clung to Burr in his hour of trial: need we say that it was a woman, the only daughter of the accused?

If there is a redeeming feature in the character of Burr, it is to be found in his love for that child. From her earliest years he had educated her with a care to which we look in vain for a parallel among his contemporaries. She grew up, in consequence, no ordinary woman. Beautiful beyond most of her sex; accomplished as few females of that day were accomplished, she displayed to her family and friends a fervour of affection which not every woman is capable of; the character of Theadosia Burr has long been regarded almost as we would regard that of a heroine of romance. Her love for her father partook of the purity of a better world; holy, deep, unchanging; it reminds us of the affection which a celestial spirit might be supposed to entertain for a parent, cast down from heaven, for sharing in the sin of the "Son of the Morning." No sooner did she hear of the arrest of her father, than she fled to his side. There is nothing in human history more touching than the hurried letters, blotted with tears, in which she announced her daily progress to Richmond; for she was too weak to travel with the rapidity of the mail. Even the character of Burr borrows a momentary halo from hers, when we peruse his replies, in which, forgetting his peril and relaxing the stern front he assumed towards his enemies, he laboured only to quiet her fears, and inspire her with confidence in his acquittal. He even writes from his prison in a tone of gayety, jestingly regretting that his accommodations are not more elegant for her reception. Once, and once only, does he melt, and that is to tell her that in the event of the worst, he will die worthy of himself.

After his trial, Burr went abroad, virtually a banished man. He was still full of his schemes against Mexico and the Spanish provinces; but in England he met with no encouragement, the nation being engaged in the Peninsular war. He afterwards visited France, where his petitions were equally disregarded, the Emperor being engrossed in the continental wars. Here his funds failed. He had no friend to apply to, and was forced to borrow, on one occasion, a couple of sous from a cigar woman on the corner of the street.

At last he returned to New York, but in how different a guise from the days of his glory! No cannon thundered at his coming, no crowd thronged along the quay. Men gazed suspiciously upon him as he walked along, or crossed the street to avoid him, as one having the pestilence. But he was not, he thought, wholly destitute. His daughter still lived, his heart yearned to clasp her to his bosom. She left Charleston, South Carolina, accordingly, to meet him. But although more than thirty years have elapsed, no tidings of the pilot boat in which she sailed have ever been received. Weeks grew into months, and months glided into years. Yet her father and husband watched in vain for her coming. Whether the vessel perished by conflagration—whether it foundered in a gale, or whether it was taken by pirates, and all on board murdered, will never be known, until the great day when the sea shall give up its dead.

It is said that this blow broke the heart of Burr, and that though in public he maintained a proud equanimity, in private, tears forced themselves down his furrowed cheeks. He lived thirty years after this event; but in his own words "felt severed from the human race." He had neither brother, nor sister, nor lineal descendant. No man called him by the endearing name of friend. The weight of fourscore years was on his brow. He was racked by disease. At last death, so long desired, came, but it is said in a miserable lodging and alone. Was there ever such a retribution?

ANONYMOUS.

II.

SECRET CORRESPONDENCE.

General Wilkinson and Burr began their correspondence in cipher about the years 1800 and 1801, near the period at which the latter ascended the chair of the Vice-Presidency. For this purpose they adopted three different ciphers.

The first is called the hieroglyphic

× 1 / Ͽ - ⊙ ◡̇ 1 ÷ ⌒̣ "∨ ⌒̣ —— ⌒̣ ○ - ∧"

○ President.

⊙ Vice-President.

÷ Secretary of State.

It was invented by General Wilkinson and Captain Campbell Smith as long ago as the year 1794, '95, or '96, for the purpose of communicating confidentially with the general officers in the Western country.

Another cipher, of a somewhat similar construction, was divised by Captain Smith in 1791, in which the hieroglyphics representing the President and Vice-President are the same with those used in the cipher of Col. Burr.

The second is denominated the *arbitrary alphabet cipher;* and was formed by Burr and Wilkinson in the year 1799 or 1800.

A	B	C	D	E	F	G	H.
—	|	/	\	∧	∨	⫲	*S.*
		1	2	3	4		
		⊤	⌊	⌋	□		

This cipher was nothing more than a substitution of characters in the place of letters which actually compose the alphabet. It was also used in figures, from one to ten.

The third is styled the *dictionary cipher;* and was adopted by them in the year 1800. The famous letters from Burr to Wilkinson, of the 22d July, 1806, delivered by Swartwout at Natchez, and its duplicate of the 29th of the same month, conveyed to Bollman, were written partly in each of these two ciphers, and partly in English. The Wilmington edition of Entick's Pocket Dictionary of 1800 served as the key, by which such parts of the letters as were written in figures were to be interpreted. For example, if the figures 3 and 4 were used, the figure 3 pointed out the *page* in the book, and 4 the *number* of the *word* intended—counting from the top in the first or second column on the page, which latter circumstance was indicated by a slight mark above or below the 4.

General Dayton's letters of the 16th and 24th July, which were forwarded in company with Burr's by Swartwout and Bollman, were written partly in hieroglyphics and the arbitrary alphabetical ciphers, above described, partly in English, but principally in Dayton's own cipher, of which the key-word is FRANCE.

It is composed in the following manner, the letters of the alphabet being numbered thus:

1	2	3	4	5	6	7	8	9	0
a	b	c	d	e	f	g	h	i	j

In order to decipher a letter or passage written in cipher, take the first letter of the key-word F, fix on the letter in the series of the alphabet; count forward from that letter as many letters as are equal to the first figure in the ciphered letter; as 8, for example, which will give I, and I will be the first letter of the first word; then take the second letter of the key word R, and in the same manner as in the first instance, count forward as many letters as are equal to the second figure; as 2, which will give the second letter T, completing the first word, *It.* Continue the same way with the ensuing letters of the key-word, till they are finished; and then begin again—thus going through the key word again and again until the letter is completed.

In the ciphered letter the figure, or aggregate of figures representing words, are separated by commas.

There was another cipher in use among some of the accomplices in this enterprise, the key-word of which was CUBA. The use of this cipher may be understood from the following scheme and explanations :—

1	C	U	B	A
2	.. d	.. v	.. c	.. b
3	.. e	.. w	.. d	.. c
4	.. f	.. x	.. e	.. d
5	.. g	.. y	.. f	.. e
6	.. h	.. z	.. g	.. f
7	.. i	.. a	.. h	.. g
8	.. j	.. b	.. i	.. h
9	.. k	.. c	.. j	.. i
10	.. l	.. d	.. k	.. j
11	.. m	.. e	.. l	.. k
12	.. n	.. f	.. m	.. l
13	.. o	.. g	.. n	.. m
14	.. p	.. h	.. o	.. n
15	.. q	.. i	.. p	.. o
16	.. r	.. j	.. q	.. p
17	.. s	.. k	.. r	.. q
18	.. t	.. l	.. s	.. r
19	.. u	.. m	.. t	.. s
20	.. v	.. n	.. u	.. t
21	.. w	.. o	.. v	.. u
22	.. x	.. p	.. w	.. v
23	.. y	.. q	.. x	.. w
24	.. z	.. r	.. y	.. x
25	.. a	.. s	.. z	.. y
26	.. b	.. t	.. a	.. z

In order to compose a letter in this species of cipher, find in the column under the first letter in the key-word, the first letter of the word which you wish to write, and the figure opposite to this letter represents the first letter of that word. To find the figure expressive of the second letter, look for that letter in the second column, and the figure opposite to that letter represents the second letter in the word. Continue in the same way with respect to the other two columns, if it be a word of three or four letters. But if it contains more than four letters, you must return to the first column and proceed in the same manner; that is, the fifth letter of the word is to be found in the first column under C; the sixth letter in the second column, and so on. Thus, if *Hope* was the first word in the epistle, look for the letter H in the first column under C, which is opposite the figure 6 as the representative of the first letter; the letter O is to be sought for in the second column, and is represented by the number 21; and so on with the letters P and E.

In the ciphered letters, the figures representing letters are separated by periods.

The reader will immediately perceive that besides *France* and *Cuba,* any other words might be used as key-words of these ciphers, according to the discretion of the writer and his correspondent. The difficulty of discovering the key to one of these ciphered letters would be still further augmented by the writer's shifting his key-word for different epistles, according to some rule previously agreed on. The difficulty would be incalculably increased, if the writer not only continues to shift his key-word, but the cipher itself.

Richmond Enquirer of 1807.

III.

THE BATTLE OF MUSKINGUM, OR DEFEAT OF THE BURRITES.

NOVEMBER 1806, BY GENERAL E. W. TUPPER.

IT has been the province of the bards in all ages, to record the glorious achievements of their warriors. The heroes of the Nile, Marengo, and Austerlitz, have had their honours recounted; and shall not those of Muskingum live, while thousands are forgotten? Yes, ye virtuous few! Ye also shall live! and millions yet unborn, while passing, shall point to the shores of Muskingum and the plains of Marietta, and say, "There fought the brave, and there the immortal fell!!" The following imitation of the "Battle of the Kegs" is offered to the public, not without its many imperfections. The writer has, in several instances, chosen to sacrifice the harmony of his rhymes to the more essential article—*truth*.

Ye jovial throng, come join the song
  I sing of glorious feats, sirs;
Of bloodless wounds, of laurels, crowns,
  Of charges, and retreats, sirs;

Of thundering guns, and honours won,
  By men of daring courage;
Of such as dine on beef and wine,
  And such as sup their porridge.

When Blanny's fleet, so snug and neat,
  Come floating down the tide, sirs,
Ahead was seen, one-eyed Clark Green,*
  To work them, or to guide, sirs.

Our General brave,† the order gave,
  "To arms! To arms! in season!
Old Blanny's boats, most careless float,
  Brim-full of death and treason!"

A few young boys, their mother's joys,
  And five men there were found, sirs,
Floating at ease—each little sees
  Or dreams of death and wound, sirs.

"Fly to the bank! on either flank!
  We'll fire from every corner;
We'll stain with blood Muskingum's flood,
  And gain immortal honour.

The cannon there shall rend the air,
  Loaded with broken spikes, boys,
While our cold lead, hurled by each head,
  Shall give the knaves the gripes, boys,

Let not maids sigh, or children cry,
  Or mothers drop a tear, boys,
I have the Baron‡ in my head,
  Therefore you've nought to fear, boys,

Now to your posts, this numerous host,
  Be manly, firm, and steady.
But do not fire, till I retire,
  And say when I am ready."

---

* A bold man, well known in those days.

† Major-general Buell.

‡ The only system of military tactics then in use in the western country among the officers, was that of Baron Steuben.

The Deputy,* courageously,
  Rode forth in power and pride, sirs;
Twitching his reins, the man of brains†
  Was posted by his side, sirs.

The men in ranks stand on the banks,
  While, distant from its border,
The active aid scours the parade,
  And gives the general order.

"First, at command, bid them to stand;
  Then, if one rascal gains out,
Or lifts his poll;—G—d d—n his soul,
  And blow the traitor's brains out."

The night was dark, silent came Clark
  With twelve or fifteen more, sirs;
While Paddy Hill, with voice most shrill
  Hooped! as was said before, sirs,

The trembling ranks, along the banks,
  Fly into Shipman's manger;
While old Clark Green, with voice serene,
  Cried, "Soldiers, there's no danger.

"Our guns, good souls, are setting poles,
  Dead hogs I'm sure can't bite you;‡
Along each keel is Indian meal;
  There's nothing here need fright you."

Out of the barn, still in alarm,
  Came fifty men, or more, sirs,
And seized each boat and other float,
  And tied them to the shore, sirs.

---

* Governor Meigs.

† Name withheld.

‡ The boats had in them hogs recently slaughtered.

This plunder rare, they sport and share,
  And each a portion grapples.
'Twas half a kneel* of Indian meal,
  And ten of Putnam's apples.†

The boats they drop to Allen's shop,
  Commanded by O'Flannon,
Where, lashed ashore, without an oar,
  They lay beneath the cannon.

This band so bold, the night being cold,
  And blacksmith's shop being handy;
Around the forge they drink and gorge
  On whisky and peach-brandy.

Two honest tars, who had some scars,
  Beheld their trepidation;
Cries Tom, "Come, Jack, let's fire a crack;
  'Twill fright them like damnation.

"Tyler they say, lies at Belpré,
  Snug in old Blanny's quarters;
Yet this pale host, tremble like ghosts,
  For fear he'll walk on waters."

No more was said, but off they sped,
  To fix what they'd begun on;
At one o'clock, firm as a rock,
  They fired the spun-yarn cannon.

Trembling and wan stood every man;
  Then bounced and shouted murder,
While Seargant Morse, squealed like a horse,
  To get the folks to order.

---

* A measure of two quarts.

† There were a few apples in the boats belonging to A. W. Putnam of Belpré.

Ten men went out, and looked about;
  A hardy set of fellows ;
Some hid in holes, behind the coals,
  And some behind the bellows.

The Cor'ner* swore, the western shore,
  He saw with muskets bristle;
Some stamp'd the ground;—'twas cannon sound,
  They heard the grape-shot whistle.

The Deputy, mounted "Old Bay,"
  When first he heard the rattle,
Then changed his course, "great men are scarce,
  I'd better keep from battle."

The General† flew, to meet the crew,
  His jacket flying loose, sirs,
Instead of sword, he seized his board;—
  Instead of hat, his goose, sirs.

"Tyler's" he cried, "on 'tother side,
  Your spikes will never do it,
The cannon's bore will hold some more,"
  Then thrust his goose into it.

Sol raised his head, cold spectres fled;
  Each man resumed his courage;
Captain O'Flan dismissed each man
  To breakfast on cold porridge.

---

* Joel Bowen.

† Buell was a tailor by trade.

IV.

BRIEF OF BLENNERHASSETT.

UNITED STATES OF AMERICA *vs.* HARMAN BLENNERHASSETT.	BRIEF on behalf of Harman Blennerhassett, confined in the Penitentiary at Richmond, Va., under an indictment for high treason.

CASE.

Introduction to Burr. Prisoner first became acquainted with Aaron Burr by a voluntary and unsolicited visit made by A. B. to prisoner at his late residence on the Ohio, in the spring of 1805. Col. Burr arrived about nightfall. He participated during the visit in the general conversation of the company; had no private interview or business with the prisoner, and he took leave about eleven o'clock at night, with his companion, Mrs. Shaw, to pursue his voyage down the river.

2. Some time in the beginning of December following, prisoner, on his return from Baltimore, received a letter from Col. Burr, couched in polite language, and expressing a regret at not having had an opportunity of improving personal acquaintance with prisoner, owing to the absence of the latter from home.

Substance of prisoner's first letter to Burr. At this time a wish on the part of the prisoner to improve his pecuniary affairs, combining with a natural desire to cultivate an acquaintance by which, he justly thought, he might so much improve his own talents and promote the interest of his children, led him, after some reflection, to write the first letter he ever addressed to the late Vice-President, expressive of a desire to be honoured with a hope of being admitted into a participation of any speculation which might, during his tour through the country, have presented itself to Col. Burr's judgment as worthy to engage his talents. In making this advance, prisoner contemplated not only a commercial enterprise or land purchase, but a military adventure was distinctly mentioned, in which prisoner would engage. A reference, however, to the original letter, or its copy in prisoner's letter-book, will show that prisoner then considered this government alive to every sentiment of indignation and resentment that he fancied it cherished against the Spanish Court, for acts of aggression and injustice committed by its troops against American citizens and the territories of the United States, and conduct by its minister and immediate representative* at the seat of government, little short of direct insult upon our Executive. Under such impressions, prisoner conceived the inevitable necessity of a speedy war with Spain, and observed in his letter to Col. Burr, that in the event of a *Spanish War*, in which case the government and country would call upon the talents, &c., of Col. Burr, the prisoner would engage with him, in any enterprise, to be undertaken for the subjugation of any of the Spanish dominions.

Burr's second visit to the island.

3. This overture, on the part of the prisoner, procured him a visit from Col. Burr at prisoner's late residence, on the Ohio, some time in the month of August, 1806. Col. Burr spent but one night

---

* Alluding to Onis, against whom a large portion of the people of the United States were deeply incensed.

in prisoner's house. Prisoner having next day rode with him to Marietta, within a mile of which place he, the prisoner, took leave of the colonel, (then on his way to Chillicothe,) and returned home. Col. Burr arrived on the island about noon, in company with Col. De Pestre and Mr. Dudley Woodbridge, jun., with whom Col. Burr had a private interview in the library, which was terminated fully an hour and a half before dinner. Some time after dinner, Col. De Pestre and Mr. Woodbridge having left the table, the subjects of conversation which had been taken up in the library, and there at the utmost dwelt upon for twenty-five minutes, were resumed, and further considered, during not more than half an hour; after which Col. Burr and the prisoner joined the company in the hall, when the conversation became and continued general till bed-time.

Went with him to Marietta, where there was no time for organizing treason or military expeditions.

4. Prisoner remained at Marietta about twenty-four hours, from which, deducting the part of time devoted to sleep, to the occupation of Col. Burr in commissioning or contracting with D. Woodbridge, to provide for him those boats and provisions that have been seized, under the orders of the government, receiving the visits of various persons that waited him at the tavern, &c., an estimate may be easily formed of how short a time the prisoner could have availed himself, to digest the projects or to contrive the means with A. Burr of executing treason against the United States, or of founding empires in other countries.

Nature of such communications as opportunity or inclination did permit A. B. actually to make.

5. From such opportunities, however, as the prisoner derived during all the private interviews afforded him, at this time, and the disclosures therein made to him with rapidity, but also with reserve, he was led to conclude, that the sentiments of a respectable

Sentiments of the people in Orleans and Mississippi Territories. Agitated and might produce revolt, which would affect the interests of the Western country, and might induce an examination by the people into the grounds of their connection with the Atlantic States, and probably produce a separation. A. B. had no concern with these things.

majority of the people in the Orleans and Mississippi Territories were disaffected to the present government, to a degree that, in Aaron Burr's opinion, would, at no very distant period, produce a revolt which would probably call in the aid of some foreign succour to support it.

That, in such an event, the States and Territories west of the Mountains would be placed in a dilemma, out of which they should withdraw, as they might be governed by an Eastern or Western ascendency of interests: that it was the colonel's opinion the discontents, particularly in the Territory of Orleans, would induce the Western country to examine the grounds and interests of its present connection with the Atlantic States, and probably induce a separation; that he, A. B., had no further concern with these things than in a speculative way; but that he thought, as well as the prisoner, that the people should be informed on the subject before they might be drawn unawares to a crisis for which they might not be prepared.

Such an event spoken of, as sooner expected than desired, by some members of the government. People of New Orleans disgusted to a degree that might induce in beginning of revolt, a seizure of bank, &c.

That a separation of the Western from the Eastern States was an event spoken of and apprehended, at the seat of government, by some of the heads of Department, which the maladministration of the country might bring about much sooner than was desired or expected; and finally, the people of New Orleans were so much disgusted with the conduct of government towards themselves, and on Spanish affairs, that he should not be surprised to hear of their beginning a revolt by seizing the Bank and Custom-house there.

MexicanSociety wanted to place A. B. at their head; he declined.

He spoke of a society of young men of that city, openly denominated the Mexican Society, seizing and shipping some French cannon lying there, for an expedition against Mexico. When at Orleans they had solicited him to lead, but he had declined to be concerned in.

Burr would not tell Blennerhassett his exact plans at all.

6. In the course of such private conversation as opportunity offered the prisoner to have with Aaron Burr, whilst on the island and at Marietta in the said month of August, 1806, prisoner naturally endeavoured to elicit from him a disclosure of some specific project, by referring to the letter of the prisoner whereof the substance is set forth in the second paragraph. But from a reserve and conciseness observable on the part of Col. Burr on such solicitation, and from entire confidence in the honour and judgment of the Ex-Vice-President, the prisoner forbore to urge particular inquiries, that seemed to be displeasing to him, from their tendency to a development of the details of his objects and his means of effecting them.

Expulsion of Spaniards from American territory, or

7. Your client, however, did not take leave of Col. Burr without matter of some satisfaction of his curiosity and interest, sufficient to engage his serious reflections on the expediency of adopting or avoiding that concern, which now seemed to be proffered to the election of the prisoner in his interests. For, after having made the prisoner the general remarks set forth in the fifth article, with the contingency of which Col. Burr declared he had no concern, but which would not be adverse to his own particular views whether they should precede or follow them, he then signified to your client, "that the expulsion of the Spaniards from the American territory then violated by them, or even an invasion of Mexico, would be

even invasion of Mexican States by A. B. to be probably agreeable to government, if either could be effected without declaring war against Spain, which might offend France.

very pleasing to the administration, if either or both could be effected without a war being declared against Spain, which would be avoided as long as possible, from parsimonious motives on the one hand, and dread of France on the other; although the then existing circumstances would, to a probable certainty, occasion its commencement before he should engage in any operation."

But such a war must take place before any operations of his plans.

Thus led to believe the government was not adverse to such designs, whilst they were kept secret till their execution should be legalized by a declaration of war, the prisoner tendered his services to Col. Burr generally.

8. At this time, your client neither sought nor received from Col. Burr any information whatever of the use or destination intended for the boats and provisions mentioned to have been contracted for with Dudley Woodbridge, jun., Art. 4, with which the prisoner had no concern, further than as he was a constituted member of the house of Dudley Woodbridge & Co., at Marietta, save that the prisoner informed Mr. Woodbridge, when the latter seemed doubtful of the sufficiency of Col. Burr's credit at New York, that the prisoner would indemnify the company for all disbursements made on account of the boats and provisions, in the event of the bills drawn for the same on New York being dishonoured.

9. Some time in the month of August or September, 1806, your client, reflecting on the information and views disclosed to him, as aforesaid, by Col. Burr, conceived the design of

Design of publishing the Querist.

publishing in the Ohio Gazette, a series of short essays, calling the attention of the people of the Western country to a subject that might engage their interests. Three or four numbers of these papers were published, exhibiting succinctly a general and relative view, in a political aspect, of the Union and the Western country, and setting forth motives of right and expediency which should induce the country west of the mountains to seek a separation from the Atlantic States in a peaceable and constitutional manner; if they should adopt the sentiments of the writer, who took the signature of Querist. The author, in making this essay on the public mind in that quarter, had no view of aggrandizement for himself, or of a political establishment for Col. Burr in the Western country, who (Burr) assured him he neither desired nor would accept any thing within the United States. Your client was actuated to make the publication by two motives only, viz., to prepare the country by a proper direction of its interests and energies for a crisis sooner or later approaching them, not from the views or operations of Col. Burr, but from the state of things on the Mississippi; at which their espousal of an eastern or western ascendency would determine their future prosperity, and to divert public attention from scrutiny into contingent plans or operations against Spain, which, whilst kept secret, government would not disapprove, but when exposed, it would be obliged to frustrate, as it had done at New York in the case of Ogden and Smith.

To prepare the people for contingencies involving their interests,

and to mask designs against Mexico, which whilst kept secret, would probably not be impeded by government, as was the case of Ogden and Smith.

10. With these views, the prisoner pledged his honour to Fairlamb, the printer of the Gazette, that he should publish nothing that would subject him to legal penalty, and the prisoner would avow himself the author whenever it might become necessary to exonerate the printer from any responsibility. In the same spirit and for the same purposes, prisoner

Fairlamb the printer, guarantied safe to publish.

communicated his design, and read the manuscript of one of the first numbers, to John and Alexander Henderson, who solemnly pledged their joint honours to the prisoner, under the sanction of hospitality in the house of said Alexander, never to disclose the name of the author or the communication he then made them, to the purport and intent that are set forth in the fifth and ninth articles.

11. Some time in the month of October, 1806, the prisoner made a visit to Lexington, Kentucky, with views of further certifying himself of the permissive progress of Aaron Burr's speculations, so far as regarded his own exertions or the observation of government. During prisoner's stay in that country, where he remained a fortnight or three weeks, he observed Burr's popularity daily increasing; heard of no jealousy or suspicions of his views or designs on the part of the government or its agents, nor from any other quarter, till a messenger had been sent to him *express* from home, stating to him that the people of Wood county had entered into communication with the President or Governor of Virginia, by forwarding to those authorities memorials or addresses expressive of alarm for the safety of the country and their liberties, which they probably represented were likely to be endangered by Col. Burr or the prisoner, of which documents the latter has never seen originals or copies, or of any answers thereto; that the inhabitants, at the instance and under the influence of Hugh Phelps, and Alexander and John Henderson, had organized a volunteer battalion of three companies, which they had armed with the arms of the militia, that they had a general muster during the prisoner's absence from home, and were expected, by the report of Peter Taylor and others, on the evening of the day of the muster, to land on the island where the prisoner's

Visit for further insight into Burr's plans into Kentucky where Burr was acquiring much popularity.

family then dwelt, and burn his house; that in all probability the prisoner and Col. Burr would be shot, if either returned to the island; and that some kiln-dried corn then preparing at the island, would be seized by the said volunteers as soon as it was put up; Dr. Joseph Spencer, of said county, having in the meantime declared that he and others regretted that they had been obliged, through fear, to sign the resolution for organizing the said volunteer association, which some others had persisted to do.

12. Agitated by this intelligence, set out for home from Lexington, Kentucky, and reached the island between one and two o'clock on the third of November, 1806. Reflecting on his way that he should be unprovided at home with any adequate means of defence to protect his family and property against the menaced outrages of a lawless multitude with arms in their hands, he was led to call on Dr. Bennet to learn such further particulars as he might have been informed of, since the express left the island for Lexington; and to provide him (the prisoner) with such aid as the Dr. could enable him to procure from his county, against any illegal and unwarrantable attack from the people of Wood county. To effect this latter object, the prisoner freely entered into a statement of the innocence and legality of every step the prisoner should take, in virtue of his concern in the speculations of Aaron Burr, observing, that the latter had completed a large land purchase of Col. Lynch; offered to the prisoner such participation in the purchase as he might desire; and expected the prisoner, with such associates as might wish to purchase or procure donations, would leave home for the country where the lands lay, on the Washita or the Red River, in the beginning of the ensuing month; that, in a political sense, Col. Burr, as well as himself, abhorred and abjured all intentions their enemies were imputing to them, of undertaking enter-

prises illegal or adverse to the United States; and declaring that neither of them ever had, or would have, any concern with the means of effecting a division of the Union, than a readiness to deliver their opinion in favour of the right of the people to effect such a measure whenever the time might arrive which should render it expedient. The prisoner, then calling the doctor's attention to his alarms for his family and property on the island, from personal enmity borne him by the people of Wood, solicited the doctor to hasten any persons he might know in his neighbourhood, who would wish to emigrate with the prisoner, to join him as soon as possible on the island, where he did not know how soon he might need their assistance to protect him from such outrages as are stated to have been then apprehended in Article 11. To these observations, made chiefly during a ride of five miles, which the doctor was induced to take, for the sake of accompanying the prisoner as far as the ferry, the doctor was pleased to reply, that if he could dispose of his place without too great a sacrifice, he should be willing to emigrate himself; that he had no doubt it would suit many persons in his neighbourhood, to whom he would speak at the muster which was to be held in a few days; that he would address to me such as he should find disposed, in the manner prisoner had directed him, i. e., provided with rifles and blankets.

13. The prisoner took leave of the doctor at the ferry, about two o'clock, P. M., on Sunday the second of November, and reached the island on the following day. On his arrival, as well as on the road between Dr. Bennet's and his own house, he found the apprehension of an attack on the island from the point of the Little Kanawha, the head-quarters of the volunteers, had by no means subsided; and was informed an attempt would be made on his person that evening. To meet this contingency, the prisoner prepared some house-arms

he had by him during ten years; and with a view to prevent it, he condescended to conciliate Mr. Phelps, the commander of the battalion, by addressing him a letter to thank him for a message he had sent to prisoner's wife some time during her husband's absence from home, for the purpose of lulling her apprehensions from the volunteers. Prisoner also solicited an interview with him, so that he might remove whatever misconception of the prisoner's conduct or intentions might have been propagated among his neighbours. But aware of Col. Phelps's predilection for jobbing and speculation, which is notorious to all who know him, and in order to procure an interview with a person who had not been in prisoner's house for nearly seven years, by which the prisoner might induce the influence of said Phelps to moderate the passions and to allay the jealousies of the ignorant and misguided—the prisoner thought it necessary to hint to him obscurely a desire to promote his interest, by some proposition which might engage his attention.

14. The letter might, or might not have had the first effect designed by it, viz., that of putting off the assault apprehended that evening on the island; but it occasioned a visit there, after a lapse of three or four days, from Col. Phelps, with whom the prisoner had a private interview, which was opened by the prisoner with a tender of thanks for the colonel's message to Mrs. Blennerhassett, during her husband's absence. The prisoner then affected to ridicule the reports which he had heard of the meditated injuries threatened his family and property from the Point;* suggested to the colonel that he suspected the other party in the country (under the influence of the Hendersons) was now becoming so strong that its leaders would probably overturn the colonel's interest, on

* The present site of Parkersburg, Va., used to be called "The Point."—W. H. S.

which alone they had hitherto depended for whatever popularity they had acquired, and cautioned the colonel against any coalition or co-operation they might seek with him, in exciting clamour or suspicion against the views or intentions of Aaron Burr or his friends, which the past conduct of the Hendersons towards him should induce him to avoid. Col. Phelps, in reply, complained much of the ill-treatment he had received from the said Hendersons. Prisoner stated his concern with Aaron Burr in a land purchase; informing the colonel that he, the prisoner, solicited or invited no person to join in the emigration, though many had voluntarily offered to do so, but added that if the colonel wished a concern for himself or his friends, that he might look to the example of General Jackson, and other characters of distinction, who, the prisoner understood, were going to join in the settlement with many associates; that as to the rumours and suspicions that had been circulated of Col. Burr, or his friends, which accused them of engaging in any thing against the laws of the United States, such were wholly groundless: but it was not unlikely that the proximity of the purchase to that part of the country where an engagement had already taken place, or might soon be expected, between General Wilkinson and the Spaniards, would engage Col. Burr and his friends in some of the earliest adventures of the war. General Jackson being already prepared to march with 1000 or 1500 of his Tennessee militia, whenever he should think himself authorized by the orders or *wishes* of the government to put that body in motion. Col. Phelps received this information with declining to embark himself, on account of his family and the unsettled state of his affairs; but said he had no doubt many young men from Wood county would be glad to go with the prisoner, to whom he (the colonel) would recommend the speculation, as he might have opportunities. The prisoner conversed with the colonel on no other topic, except some general propositions for renting the prisoner's place by the colonel's son-in-law, Thomas Creel.

15. The prisoner, however, still continuing to receive daily assurances that the people from the Point were determined to seize and destroy his corn on the island, as well as the boats building on the Muskingum river, which were to convey his family and friends, with their provisions and necessaries to the Mississippi, thought it prudent to write to Dr. Bennet, requesting him to lend him ten or twenty guns for protection. The object of the prisoner being to resist illegal violence offered to him and his friends in their legal pursuits, he conceived he might correctly borrow rifles, the private property of individuals, or even the arms of the militia, whilst they were not wanted between days of muster, to enable him to resist an apprehended outrage on the laws of the country, in the persons of the prisoner and his friends. The doctor replied, that the arms of the militia were in the charge and under the control of the colonel, and he could procure no others.

16. Prisoner was occupied himself with preparations for his removal with his family and friends from the island, which he took every public opportunity to declare would take place from the 8th to the 10th of the next month of December, 1806, generally telling the applicants who were to go with him, to provide themselves with a rifle and blanket, but accepting the offers of many as associates without either; soliciting no man, nor offering wages or bounties to any; preparing and providing no military stores, or implements of war whatever—unless corn-meal, flour, whisky, and pork be received as such—until the latter part of November, when he had an interview with Mr. Graham at Marietta.

17. Your client, in virtue of a slight acquaintance he had formed in Kentucky, in 1801, with Mr. G., and under an im-

pression that he also was concerned in some of the speculations of Aaron Burr, visited him soon after his arrival, and was received with much ceremony and coldness. Mr. G. described the government as embarrassed by the variety and contradictory matter of statements which had been forwarded from various parts of the western country, of the equipments then providing on the Ohio and Muskingum, some representing them more, others less extensive, but all conveying a suspicion that they were destined for an attack on New Orleans, an invasion of Mexico, or for transporting emigrants, with their effects, to Col. Burr's Washita purchase; that, however, their real destination was probably New Orleans or Mexico, rather than the Washita. Mr. G. then observed, as he said, in an official character, that he had it in charge to collect such information as might enable the government to stop any military expedition, if such was intended; and in an official character he added, he would advise prisoner, if he was concerned in such designs, to withdraw from them.

18. To these observations, Mr. G. was answered by the prisoner, that the latter could not suppose the government disposed to molest individuals not offending against any law, and avowing a lawful object of their pursuits; that the prisoner, although he had no objection to avow and declare to Mr. G., as he had done to every other person, that he was concerned with Col. Burr in a land purchase, whither he should undertake a journey on the 8th or 10th of December, with such friends, from the number of sixty to one hundred, as might be ready to accompany him; would not condescend to answer interrogatories tending to charge him with being concerned in any illegal enterprise; that the commencement and progress of this journey should be innocent and peaceful, unless it were interrupted by illegal insult or violence, which should be repelled with those rifles with which he had gene-

rally directed his friends to provide themselves; and that he hoped the government, or its agents, had no wish or design to commit a wanton trespass upon men peaceably pursuing speculations, which, because, forsooth, their details were not exposed to the world, (owing to the fear of jealousy and malice of individuals who would not be permitted to participate in them,) had invoked the suspicion of government.

19. Previous to making these observations to Mr. G., your client showed him a letter, of which he offered him a copy, from Col. Burr, dated from Lexington or Frankfort in Kentucky, acquainting the prisoner with the institution of a criminal prosecution against him (Burr) by Mr. Davis, the United States Attorney for the Kentucky District, where Col. Burr observed the detention he should thereby suffer, would retard the establishment of the Washita settlement. Mr. G. dined in company with your client the same day. At table he was assured, on inquiry made by him, that your client would take his wife and family with him down the river. After dinner, your client invited Mr. G. to his room, where he observed, he had called him up again to offer him a copy of the aforesaid letter from Col. Burr, and to trouble him to state over again, in order to prevent any misunderstanding of the intentions of government, whatever official warnings he had to give, that prisoner might communicate them to Col. Burr and his friends, whose duty it would be to regulate their conduct thereby. Mr. G. then replied, that the prisoner might inform Col. Burr "the *constituted authorities* of the country would be expected on the part of the general government, to stop his boats, if they carried an unusual number of men, armed in an unusual manner." Your client then asked him whether more or less single men, or married men, accompanying your client, to the number of from sixty to one hundred, in sixteen or seventeen boats—generally taking their

rifles with them, but not their families at such a season of the year, would constitute such a party, and armed in such a manner, as would expose them to the obstruction he threatened? To this he answered, "He supposed not, though it appeared unusual and suspicious for such numbers to go so far to settle a new country without their families."

20. The prisoner now thought he had taken leave of this personage, perfectly understanding both himself and the government. On the contrary, your client, on his return in a day or two to Marietta, learned with surprise that this envoy-extraordinary of executive vigilance could not delay a moment to cool the zeal of his mission, by plunging it red-hot into those intrigues which your client's letter to Phelps, &c. had lately somewhat stagnated in Wood county. Laved and refreshed in these pellucid waters, he follows their meanders in quest of that fountain from which they issue, which, like the source of Alcinous, is hid in mystery and darkness. Arrived at the Temple erected to Honour and Hospitality, in Beech Park,* on the banks of the Little Kanawha, he is received in the vestibule by John and Alexander Henderson, the consecrated ministers of those divinities. A libation is now ordained to ancient friendship and the household gods. Another is next proposed to the tutelary deities of the place, "Hold!" cries the envoy of suspicion, "the rites of Honour and Hospitality may be administered by their votaries in these sequestered wilds. But I will never participate in such mummery before that altar on which you have sacrificed to treason and to Burr!" His brother priests are now dismayed and almost petrified. "Yes!" continues the ambassador, "the safety of the State demands a greater sacrifice to liberty.

* Alluding to the house of Henderson, the chief witness of the government at the trial of Burr.

Now purge ye of the charge committed to your keeping, of all the crimes intended to be perpetrated against your country." In vain the distracted brothers declare, "No secrets of a dangerous nature were intrusted to their sanctum—they were innocent and submitted also by him who trusted them, to sanction in the breast of an aged parent." "Say you parent, innocent secrets, and submitted for sanction to the breast of a parent? Why not then disclose them to the parent of the State. I am his minister and will take charge of them!"

21. Your client hopes the last paragraph may not displease, by its length or obscurity. The style he has there fallen into was insensibly suggested and protracted by his reflections on the intelligence he received from Morgan Neville, Esquire,* that it cost Mr. Secretary Graham no little labour to work the Hendersons up to break the seal of that Honour and Hospitality which the prisoner imagined they would preserve inviolate, when he made confidential communications to them, and through them to their father, to the effect set forth in the 5th and 9th Articles.— *Wallace's "Blennerhassett."*

---

* The elegant author of "Mike Fink, or the last of the Boatmen."

THE END.

www.ingramcontent.com/pod-product-compliance
Lightning Source LLC
LaVergne TN
LVHW012328100826
845148LV00017B/394

* 9 7 8 1 4 2 5 5 2 0 5 0 2 *